from here to district six:
with new poetry, pros

for my people and their people's people–still searching
to my mother, father and my sisters looking for home
to the griots and griottes who continue to inspire me
and to the exile in all of us
viva the moffies!

Also by Norman G. Kester:

Liberating Minds

I, Moffie: A Queer South African Memoir (unpublished)

Poetry, Prose, Essays and Memoir

from here to district six

Plays

The Family

from here to district six
a south african
memoir with new
poetry, prose and
other writings

Norman G. Kester

DISTRICT SIX PRESS

Toronto • Canada

Copy edited by Elizabeth Phinney
Cover art and design by Brian Lam
First edition, March 2000

Canadian Cataloguing in Publication Data

Kester, Norman G., 1962-
From here to District Six: a South African memoir with new poetry, prose and and other writings
Includes bibliographical references.
ISBN 0-9686342-0-6

1. Kester, Norman G., 1962-   -Literary collections. 2. South Africa–Literary collections. 3. Apartheid–South Africa–Literary collections. 4. Colored People (South Africa)–Literary Collections . 5. Black Canadians–Literary collections.* 6. Gay men's writings, Canadian (English).* 7. Exiles' writings, African (English). I. Title.

PS8571.E785F76 2000   C818'.5409   C99-932863-8
PR9199.3.K4278F76 2000

DISTRICT SIX PRESS, ngkester@total.net
c/o 77 Huntley Street, Suite 2412, Toronto, Ontario, Canada M4Y 2P3

umuntu ngununtu ngabantu

(a person is a person through persons)

–Xhosa proverb

...the poet appropriates the voice of the people
and full burden of their memory

–Wole Soyinka, *The Burden of Memory*

It was linked in some way to the creative function,
the dreamer of new dreams; and the essential ingredient
in creativity is *to create* and let the dream fly away...

–Bessie Head, in speaking of her
greatest literary work, *A Question of Power*

death makes us all poets, for it is
the heart which speaks, cries

CONTENTS

FOREWORD

This book takes me back to years and years of struggling for justice and freedom for black people in my country, South Africa. Here are my meaningful memories gleaned from the weary mind and body of a black gay activist:

I suppose that I was aware of my sexuality at the earliest time of my life. Finally, when I was in high school, I came to realize that my feelings were genuine. Yes, I was *gay* and I had to live with it. I decided to tell my parents. My mother took it very hard but I was very glad that she did not chase me out of the house. My stepfather was very understanding and supportive. He was a chef in a five-star hotel in Jo'burg and he explained to my mother that he knew many gay men who always went to the hotel and many of them were successful businessmen.

Elizabeth (Mother) did not buy the whole story. She believed that I could be "cured" from my "illness." Ja, Mother believed that I was very sick and she took drastic action. Some of the things she did were offensive to me, especially the weekly visits to the psychiatrist and being taken to the isangomas, or traditional African healers, who even told me to drink a potion mixed with my sister's urine! It took a very long struggle and time before my mother came to terms with accepting my sexuality, and during this struggle, I twice attempted to take my own life. I am glad that I did not succeed, as my mission of helping other people would have not have been accomplished.

My first lover was a white man, but marriages between black and white people were not allowed under the *Mixed Marriages Act*. Now you can imagine how difficult it was for gay men because homosexuality was a punishable offence and you could be locked up in prison. Three years maximum.

André and I were never very happy about the way we were forced to lead our life. I lived in the Township of Sebokeng and he lived in the white-only suburbs. There was no way that we could live together. I had to pretend that I was working for Baas André: we were a boy and a master to outsiders, not lovers. I grew tired for even he was not supportive of my struggle against apartheid. He was very afraid that I would be arrested, banned or detained without trial, but most of all he was scared that he would be incriminated should the police know that he was my friend. Our relationship soon ended. He did not understand that there was a war on and my brothers and sistahs were fighting: my conscience failed to allow me to stand back and merely watch what was going on around me.

Unlike many activists, I remained in South Africa and had to fight apartheid–a monster with wings and legs, devouring us, maiming us, jailing us and killing us. With others, I was arrested on the 23rd of September 1984, and little did I know that I was going to be charged with high treason, terrorism, murder and furthering the aims of the banned African National Congress and South African Communist Party. I had been detained several times before like many under Section 29 of the *Internal Security Act*. It allowed the police to detain you for about six months for interrogation. If you were lucky you would be released. But if they felt they had not gained any information from you, your detention without trial would be extended for another six months or more. And this is what happened to me. I was in detention without trial for eighteen months and charged together with twenty-one other activists, mostly from the Vaal Triangle. After three long, hard years, I was released on bail in June

1987–and acquitted from the Delmas Treason Trial in November. My struggle was hard because just before I was arrested everything was beginning to take shape for black lesbians and gay men in the township.

There was this one man who was very feminine from our neighbourhood in Sebokeng. Everybody despised, hated and teased him. Our parents warned us against him, but as children we did not understand, and we were not allowed to ask why. Children were not supposed to ask those kinds of questions. We were told to do things and asked only to listen. The man disappeared from our township, and no one knew where he went to. Even now, we don't know what happened to him.

In August 1982, I wrote a letter to the *Golden City Post* calling for black lesbians and gays to come out and start a support group after I joined the Gay Association of South Africa (GASA). I was astonished to see that within a few days I was loaded with many letters from black gay men and lesbians from all over the neighbouring states. There were about seventy people at the first meeting and so we resolved to start a support group, which we called the Saturday Group.

But all was not well. It was not too long before members of GASA started showing some signs of disapproval of our newly found support group. They started complaining about the noise and littering we were "causing" at the GASA offices. Due to the unwelcoming attitude of the white gay men towards us, we had no choice but to resign en masse from the organization. I, however, did not leave as I had a strong feeling that I could change the situation from within. I guess I was wrong. White people could not change: they had everything, all of the comforts, and enjoyed the fruits of apartheid. They were very well off, and they did not want to be involved with fighting against a system that gave them social, economic and political privilege.

There was one incident that I shall never forget. In September 1982, GASA organized a trip to the zoo in Pretoria. After we had been assured that blacks would not be chased away, three of my friends and I decided to go with the rest of the members. We were given lifts to Pretoria, and on arrrival to the zoo, we were told, "Sorry, blacks are not allowed in." Maybe they were afraid that we would steal the lions or perhaps eat the elephants. After some time trying and failing to discuss and argue about the problem with guards at the zoo, our white members of GASA suggested that blacks should wait at the car park as they wanted to explore the beauty of the zoo. I was too offended and refused to remain and just walked freely, all by myself. I felt so alone, so terribly hurt. My defiant action angered members of GASA and soon I was called to a disciplinary meeting in which I was suspended. I remember writing from prison in July 1987 that GASA had fabricated evidence that it was a "multiracial organization" fighting apartheid. In fact, in some cases it was collaborating with the the police. It would later die a welcome death in the end.

Nothing was exciting for us in the townships around the country. We did not have meeting places for black gay men and lesbians until one day a lady by the name of Lee, who owned a shebeen in Soweto, invited us there. We were very excited about the idea and we used the shebeen as a community place, to talk about our issues and ideas. It served also as the only place of entertainment for black gay men in the area. However, it was soon raided by the police who arrested the clientele and even the owner.

Full of excitement, I remember getting up at 5 a.m. and standing in a line two kilometres long to vote for the first time in 1994. All of us had waited so long–all of our lives–for this day, and many old people stood in line for hours! Gay and Lesbian Organization of Witwatersrand (GLOW), the only black and non-racial gay and lesbian organization in the country which I founded asked all of the political parties in the country about their position on issues relating to lesbians and gay men. The leader of the Pan African Congress said that homosexuality was "un-African." The National Party said that animals and minors were examples of "orientation." But the ANC gave us a strong affirmative response to work for change. A bill of rights was adopted, guaranteeing the protection of gay and lesbian people, and this is now part of our constitution.

There is still much to do in the new, democratic South Africa. As President Mandela said–you don't just wake up one day and have a democracy. Everyone must work hard to make it happen. The shacks of the people might soon disappear. It feels like we are finally free with a government that rules for the people. Being gay or lesbian does not mean losing one's self-respect in South Africa. Being human, connecting with other human beings compassionately and understanding that my humanity is bound up in your humanity–this is the African idea of ubuntu though it is difficult to describe–is really what unites us, not our ethnic or sexual make-up.

As I, too, am thinking about my life, I wonder if I shall see the twenty-first century. My health situation due to my AIDS status has not been good, and many Africans can ill-afford the AIDS cocktails that are available to those in the West and that American companies deny us. There is still much to do. We have our own unfinished business of building bridges together, rising from the ashes of apartheid, all of us, blacks, coloureds and whites–all who feel disempowered, all who suffered or caused suffering. My life has been full of possibility and wonder, but it has also been full of loss. Those who read this work will see its brutal honesty and truth. Its rage. Ag, man we are all so vulnerable; we must all move on–and *live*.

Tseko Simon Nkoli
Yeoville, South Africa, March 1998

Tseko Simon Nkoli (26 November 1957-30 November 1998) was an active member of the United Democratic Front and Congress of South African Students during apartheid. He became an international spokesman for the gay and lesbian rights movement there and abroad, founding the Gay and Lesbian Organization of the Witswatersrand (GLOW), the Township AIDS Project (TAP) and the National Coalition for Lesbian and Gay Equality (NCLGE). As a board member of the International Lesbian and Gay Association, Nkoli wished for its conference to be held in South Africa–for the first time. This wish was realized in October of 1999. Nkoli achieved much during his short lifetime, winning international praise. A Hillbrow street corner was named after him finally, a first for a black gay South African.

INTRODUCTION

"...you can take the people out of the heart of District Six, ou pellie, but
you'll never take District Six out of the heart of the people."

–District Six Resident, 1966

We'd leave South Africa in 1969–without Mummy. I have often said that writing
and performing poetry is like the pain of living and dying all at once. *from here to
district six* is about searching for *home* and mother/land, for my South African identity, culture and past long buried by living in this country. Although I began an
unpublished memoir after the final death of my mother on this theme, it was not
published for a variety of reasons. It has seemed that for thirty years I have wanted
to say these things found in my book–to brothers and sisters here and in South Africa,
to family and friends. Some prose found in *I, Moffie* has been edited and included in
this work, and so to is Nkoli's foreword. With sadness, he succumbed to AIDS hero-
ically in November of 1998. Simon was a casuality like so many others who
continue to live and struggle with the disease in South Africa and the rest of the
continent, but he still managed to send me his meaningful piece despite his failing
health situation. I always knew our paths would cross one day, and so I am indeed
grateful that Simon could muster the energy to complete his piece. Nkoli's voice
echoes certain universal truths about his life, the lives of all disenfranchised people of
the world. Maybe we did "know" each other, albeit in different ways.

We are all too busy in a city of anthills to think about the reality of life, as I heard
a friend once say, or maybe we don't want to go that deeply, probe that far as we are
afraid to look at ourselves in the mirror–finally, truthfully. The poet is unafraid to
think and write of these things, because if he does not, then who will? Apartheid has
not yet ended in South Africa: it has simply taken on a new form, and black Africans
in the country are still by and largely uneducated, impoverished and greatly underem-
ployed. Some 64,000 women and young girls are raped daily, and this is three times
higher than in the United States. This figure reveals a society that is indeed troubled.
Incidents of police violence and deaths of those jailed is very high. Although the
past continues to haunt us, it may also tell us where our future lies.

Cape coloureds or people of mixed race with whom my family is associated have
their early beginnings in District Six, which began with the full emancipation of the
slaves arriving in 1834. Most came from the Dutch East Indies, including the
Malayan archipelago, Sri Lanka, India, as well as Madagascar. The Khoisan or
"bushmen" were the first inhabitants of the Cape area before the Dutch colonialists
brutally exterminated them. Mixing took place over many generations–first between
white men and slave women or slave men and Khoikhoi or San women–producing
the coloured people. From 1966 to the early 1980s the apartheid government forcibly
removed some 60,000 people–mostly coloured families from District Six, which was
declared a "white area"–and relocated them on the barren Cape Flats. Even though it
remains nearly a wasteland, District Six became an ingrained symbol against the
brutality of apartheid, indeed a symbol of resistance and hope for freedom for all
South Africans. This brings to mind Africville's demolishment in Canada and the
oppression suffered by First Nations peoples by the government throughout this country's history. Moffie life was rich in District Six, despite its deperation and poverty.
"Gays," who would meet and cruise at bioscopes (cinemas) or at lavish home parties,
would jump off vans and do the Charleston to entice people to their marvellous

competitions at the Embassador Club where they performed in lavish ballroom costumes. They lived at home, helped their poor families and took the children to school.

A culture of mourning describes the life of the outcast, the oppressed, the dispossessed. We mourn to live. Coloured people, I have read and maybe understood, were never accepted by the Afrikaner Nationalists, and will probably not be boistered by an ANC government that has even gone so far as to introduce legislation that would outlaw freedom of speech. History has shown that we have been colonized, othered, and belittled. Many coloureds have felt that Affirmative Action–a policy adopted by the ANC government to create jobs for Africans over other racial groups–has worked against them. Coloureds were given preferential treatment over Africans in the apartheid years, but they were also relegated to an underclass with little control over their lives. Does that mean we are forever trapped, caught in the middle, with no place to go? Maybe that is still how I see my self: *without* a home. To not properly define myself–am I African, am I coloured or just "mixed"?–is the brutal question I must face once and for all. It is also the question that faces all South Africans as they debate their renewed future. *But in the final end we mourned Mummy–always.* In a sense our mourning was also a deep sense of yearning, of spiritual longing for home, culture and country.

I wanted to become a *whole* person again when I undertook my memoir project. My poetry, the restful waters, carries me back to the place of my birth, and even to District Six in Cape Town, which is akin to the spiritual heartland of being coloured and South African. And when I depart this world, my ashes will be sprinkled off the deep cradling sea at Table Bay.

We still have a lot to learn and understand from those in the Third World–Canada's First Nations peoples, who still see their circle as a way of life, South Africa's Zulus and Mexico's many indigenous peoples, who have regarded the Canada-U.S. Free Trade Agreement as a "death" to their way of life. All must long for their past traditions, and fear that Western imperialist ways will forever destroy their native culture.

With the advent of the twenty-first century, I have thought that it is about the power of taking our lives into our own hands. It is not about globalism and capitalism in all of its ugly forms, or the slavery of being tied to bureaucracy. It is about recreating ourselves–*with* our families. It means looking within ourselves, redefining our culture and understanding that we are all connected as human beings, that the taal we speak will be the same. And for Africa, it means a cultural renaissance of sorts. For "queers" of African descent, let us no longer be slaves of our past, but rejoice in our spiritual future with our brothers and sisters here and in the diaspora.

As Nikki Giovanni has written, "There is no difference between the warrior, the poet and the people." We will get beyond just being called moffies, ngochani, moataona, bulldagger, anti-man, batty man and zami. It was poet and essayist Audre Lorde herself who said that "our silences will not protect us." Our activism and existence has helped us not only to celebrate who we are but to also liberate each other, even those who oppress us.

from here to district six attempts to speak of national and personal forgiveness, but at the same time we who were oppressed by Apartheid must ask ourselves: can we forgive Them–white Afrikaners–whom some would call "the liars of our history"–for their cruelty, for murdering and separating our families, for stealing our future? Can native and black Canadians forgive whites for Oka, for the Yonge Street Riots, for Africville? Can I finally forgive my father for "taking us" from our mother/land, even the gay community, really the "ghettoized life"–which still oppresses me, and those who do not fit in? If we do not forgive Them, and ourselves–we cannot move on. *Live*, be free. Without forgiveness, Africa may not have a future or renaissance.

Coloured South Africans must learn to look to the future, to develop their own proud past. They must rise from the evil and ashes of apartheid. Saying that the new South Africa is non-racial is beside the point. It does not mean that coloured poeple no longer exist. They *do*. We have developed our own unique cultural institutions and ideas over centuries–values which have been unquestionably shaped by our rich African past–which will carry us into liberation and a prosperous future so that that the next generation may carry on. Coloured citizens, as citizens of Africa, must begin the twenty-first century, not from a position of powerlessness, fear or abandon-ment, but optimism and immense achievement. We must learn to shrug off our colo-nized past, both internal and external.

The Encyclopedia of the Future finally revealed what the next century might hold for us: "Africans will turn to literature and the arts (drawing upon strong cultural traditions merging poetry, song, dance and the life of the individual and society) as important linkages for global linkages." This augers well for our cultural survival–our future, and the planet's future.

I give gratitude for the love of my sisters and family, Tseko Simon Nkoli, the Jamaican-Canadian poet Courtnay McFarlane whom I performed with at *too blk/too large*! (a poetry reading in Toronto in 1998 to celebrate the life of Simon Nkoli), the staff of the Mississauga Library System–especially its Central Library and librarian James B. Drake, Petro Lombard at the South African State Library in Pretoria, the faithful support of artist-friend Brian Lam, filmmaker Moze Mossanen and his sister, photographer Mimi Mossanen, Dr. Rozena Maart of Guelph University, a South African-Canadian academic whose family was forced out of District Six, and finally, York University humanities scholar and cultural critic Dr. Rinaldo Walcott.

The Hausa have a saying: "Wherever you see a road it leads to a house." I wanted to know the roots of my family's painful separation and past. *Truth. Forgiveness. Reconciliation. Love.* That is what *I,* what we all want, finally. Ja.

Norman G. Kester
Toronto, Canada, November 1999

in the early fall of my spoiled childhood

i, blanche

My life here, well, it goes on. I have no blaady privacy man. No privacy. No time to think and be by myself. I am being watched. They are watching me. The security police. But they will not find me out. I'm wiser than that. No one knows that I write about this in my diary, or about the dark demons that plague me incessantly. I have snakes in my stomach and feel naar.

Victor looks after me, even though we are separated by sleeping areas for coloureds and Africans. No one knows of our dear friendship. He was also married, now he is here. He makes sure no one hurts me–the other men, here. Victor is pleasant to talk to. He tells me stories of his life as a newspaperman in Jo'burg. Was he at *The World**, and was he from a black location or township? Then I think he told me that his wife passed away. My sympathy. Had to stay with his children in town when his nerves were bad. Now he's here. I'm glad that I found him. But we must be careful not to be seen together, or even sit together for fear that the sisters and white doctors will see us do this. He has his off days like me. I don't like being with so many sick people. I don't know why men who are common loafers and criminals are also kept here. They and some of the women steal my clothes. Violet tells me to give her my nice dresses and jerseys to take home with her. Too dear to buy new clothes everytime my things are buggerall stolen, she says.

I've noticed that the large room is usually clean, but now and then I'd just stand around gazing at my sleeping area. It was painted rather plainly and some of the boarders were half-clothed and unable to sign their names, refusing to bathe, making the ward smell bad. Even asking that the doors and windows be kept open as long as time permits during the summer blazes would do no good to alleviate the stench of human odour. That smell is as close as death.

The sisters frequently become mad if they see us make a mess, especially where we sleep. I'm sure that they take our clothes and things. They haven't much else for their families.

My bed is barely able to hold my small body. It is placed in a row of other beds close to each other, and sometimes I wonder why I do not have my own bit of sleeping area, just as I had at Sterkfontein Hospital. The blankets are thin and navy blue, and we take them off for wollen ones in the winter. My bunk mates keep me company, and say nice things to me. "Blanche, man, stop thinking of your children. You must go on with life, and hope that one day you shall see them, né!" they say to me motheringly.

I have begun to sew pockets in my sweater, especially for the cold winter winds. The harsh winds. I can keep my writing journal, pen, postal stamps and, sometimes, the little bit of lipstick and some food that I take from the warder's lounge. What would I ever do without my prayer book which I read daily? Violet tells me I can find sustenance by looking at this book whenever my nerves overtake me. I keep praying to myself but can only think of my four little ones.

---

* *The World* was soon banned by the Nationalist government in 1977.

Victor, when he isn't busy with his duties, will sit by me, away from everyone else. The newspaper occupies his attention. We quietly sit outside near the large tree. He with his reading, me with mine, or my writing. Sometimes all that I have to do is look nicely at his paper, then he understands I want to read it to see what is happening in the rest of the world, or in Jo'burg. He makes me happy, ja–just being next to him. "I am your protector, Blanche. As long as I am here, no harm will come to you. I promise you that," he tells me on the days when he wants to chat with me. "This place is not fit for human beings," he reminds me as we pass our time together. It was his daughter who put him here. What kind of person is she? Who would do such a cruel thing–to a father?

"You want some sweets, Blanche?" Victor asks me, as he closes his newspaper. I looked as he held his hands outward, coffee-coloured from the hot sun. "Thank you," I said kindly, as I took a shiny one and placed it into my mouth. The sugary mint taste reminded me of the Christmas holidays, and even of the time of De Beers each December when me and my family would be treated to a springbok meal and the children would get a special gift from Father Christmas. There was that snap of all of them including her husband, posed in front of that large pine tree. Those days were filled with joy, for she remembered her children, the exact time of their births and what ailed them, including their taste for certain foods she had prepared with Winnie, the maid.

"You never told me about your relatives, much," I say to Victor, "or even about your parents."
"If you must know, my name is really Makhaya, Blanche, and my father's father was a Mphabele–an African. My grandmother died without ever having carried a pass. But now my young nephews fear wearing a "Black is Beautiful" T-shirt. That's how things are these days." "Things for us aren't so good either," I replied. "We're moved to isolated areas and can't afford to bus to work. Even the coloured usherettes working in the white bioscopes in Jo'burg were told that, to work there, they must *not* look at the white films. Ja, they must turn their eyes away from the screens as if white life were too beautiful, too sacred for us poor coloureds to view, to desire."

Victor listens intently, shaking his head, glasses now off from his tired eyes. "Ja, Blanche–my name was changed to hide my true identity, but I believe in the African ways even though this has been driven out of us by the government."
"What do you mean?"
"I've been taken to an African healer, an isangoma to help drive the evil from me. My nerves, you know..."
"Ja, but...did this work?"

Victor puts down his paper again. "I was told by the isangoma that I might be possessed by swikwembus: these are ancestral spirits. She cast holy bones from her small goatskin bag as we sat in a circle around her. She then asked me first to blow into the bag, before she threw the bones onto the ground. Her old eyes looked deeply at what they meant and later she sucked the evil spirits from my body. It was blaady costly, man. I felt right for some time, until my daughter told me that she was bringing me here."

Raising my eyebrows, I thought a bit. "Sounds like witchcraft to me!"

"What's so different about the white doctor's witchcraft? The isangoma told me the bones said I had been an unkind and uncaring husband to my wife when she died. So now I was supposed to pray to her spirit everyday. Herbal medicines were given to me to drink and later, something was smeared over my body."

"Anything is possible jong. Look at me here at the sanitorium. It has got me nowhere!"

"Maybe you are running away."

"Running away from what?"

"Tragedy. Life. The madness of apartheid."

"Who wouldn't?" I answered back quickly. "He left me with nothing on my back. I miss my children as much as I miss my freedom. The country is sick. We are all sick."

"The mother has the sacred element, Blanche. Don't lose all hope. Somehow your children will come back to you. At least you can pass, man."

I scolded him. "Pass for what?" But he was right. There was straight hair in the family.

He took to his reading again. And I wrote a letter to my sister, thinking of the lovely braais, the children and Mary. Many silent minutes passed between us, and then looking up into the open skies he said, as if speaking to himself, "Maybe we need the spirit of Nongqause to make us sacrifice our lives to drive away those who wear trousers–the white men who have destroyed our society. The dead would surely rise and return our rightful land."

"Or should we use the spear?" I asked. It was completely out of character.

There was news of how things were becoming harder for us to live in South Africa. A white man and a coloured woman, it was reported, were tried for kissing. The court was in a frenzy over the question of whether the kiss was platonic or passionate. *Would Victor and I also be tried, I thought?* I quickly wanted to forget my anxious feelings.

"I am not a social pusher, but it is people who make these unjust laws, Victor. They are evil, not Christian." I said this to him as we walked, not closely together, but away, so that no one would see. We talked about whom in our families had left the country rather than stay and exist in such grave conditions.

***

The asylum offered Blanche a chance to escape social conventions, even existing taboos. Everyone seemed equal here. As if by going mad, apartheid could disappear, and normality return. But it had not. She was only reminded that it was her fair skin that brought favours, many of which she declined. She despised her "whiteness"–and so called closeness to godliness, righteousness–and what whites stood for. She was not one of them, and being coloured made her all the more uncomfortable, like a dog without a home.

In the heat of the midday sun, she took her walks in the large trees past the main building, close to the apricot and peach tree orchard. She always walked by herself where she could glance at the open skies before her. Hear the orangebreasted waxbills as they flew in and out of the veld, looking for a place to bathe. Their distinctive voice–a *trip-trip-trip*–pierce the distance every now and then. Life was joyous in their company. She smelled the flowers, their hypnotic scent. She dreamed she was a flower, free and alone. The sun was upon her, the rain, too–falling and gently caressing her, falling and gently caressing her.

Flowers in a field covered her, nearly completely. Maybe death was like this. Sweet death. Each beautiful flower was one of her children: they appeared each spring, came to full life in the scorching heat of the summer, and then disappeared slowly as the winter rains approached. She looked at nearly each one, just as she might look over her children. Each died graceful, wilted deaths, only to repeat their life once again. Blanche thought of herself as a lonely tree, sheltering none of her flowers around her, rubbing up to her. The sun was strong. It touched her. She shaded her hot cheeks and burning eyes with her brown hands from its deathly heat. Undoing her jersey, hands stroked across her heaving breasts. Fingers travelled toward the place that gave her pleasure. She rubbed herself and felt soaked down there, as if time had stopped and each second was an uneasy pleasure too breathtaking to describe.

Her thoughts were not always as carefree as this. Especially after the incident many months past: a man asked if she wanted to come to his sleeping room. He had given her some things before and this time he forced himself on her, pinning her small frame with his heavy weight onto the bed in the room. She looked away from him, from his demonic eyes as he spread her legs apart with his strong legs. His heavy belly dug into her thin frame like a porcupine on a hare. Weakness overcame her. As she eyed the rise of the clouds in the distance from the corner of the window in the ward, she could only think of Victor. Men were animals. She soon rushed to her bed and tears could not stop. All who loved her had left her. She woke to wash herself several times, to get his stench off of her body before anyone could sense what had happened. The thought of killing the man soon crossed her mind. Of taking a knife to him. But her gentle heart was not strong enough, and the God whom she prayed to each night as the sun set spoke of forgiveness. Forgetting. But how could she when her heart cried anger?

I

I wouldn't speak to Victor for many days. I couldn't tell him what had happened to me. I trusted him so much and admired him because he didn't take to drink. But to say something might cause me trouble, and I didn't know if the sisters would believe me. It felt like weeks before I could muster the energy to live again in this blaady place for lunatics, to speak to him as a friend after the verkragting–when I was violated. Secretly, I think that he suspected that some grave tragedy had befallen me. He'd look into my eyes only for me to glance down casually at my journal. Weep deep inside. Weep for me and my kinders. One day, he sat beside me and surprised me with some wild orange and yellow daisies he had picked on the grounds somewhere. It brought me a bit of happiness, even tenderness.

The sun seems to brighten everything including Victor's dark hazel eyes. He wears clean pressed clothes, which his daughter brings to him weekly, and takes care of himself unlike some of the other men here. Over the last few weeks he has told me that he is feeling much better.

"What kind of name is Blanche?" he asked me as we sat alone on the grounds of the hospital. "It means *white*–in French,"–I replied. He then politely kissed me. I didn't know how to respond. It happened so quickly, outside under the shade of the Bodhi tree, as we usually sit together by ourselves, out of sight, while we read and just enjoy each other's quiet company. He kissed me not just once but a few times. I was getting all skaam as he held me and nuzzled his warm face in my bosom. But would anyone see us? Would they, and report us?

"You are a mooi, Blanche. Beautiful. I like you, né," he said, as he put his paper aside and caressed me, even undoing my jersey a bit, then stopping as gently as he began. "You are simple, but there is a warm unspokeness about you that is alluring as the swirling soothing seafoam at the Cape. And a sadness in your eyes that one does know how to paint." I was weak for human warmth from him, but I am a stranger to love. His eyes caught a glimpse of the strap of my brassiere, while his anxious fingers fumbled with my clothes. I didn't stop him; it felt right. We looked about us. Danger was everywhere. For some strange reason all that I could think of while he did this to me was about my children. Our lives, distant, distant, apart.

I'm sad as he is to leave soon. I know and I'm unsure what to say to him about it. We've only known each other for a few months and already my feelings for him are strong. Controlling everything inside is impossible; flowers bloom but they are silent. It is his constant friendship and words of kindness and wisdom that I will miss dearly. Endless reportings in the country's newspapers of the immorality cases come to mind though. Fear overpowering crippled minds.

O most kind and gracious Father, I confess unto Thee that I have sinned in thought, word and deed, through my fault, my own most grievous fault; and I beseech Thee, by the merits of our Lord Jesus Christ, whose Name we bear and in whose merits alone we trust, to create in us a clean heart and renew in us a right spirit, to give us the grace of true repentance, and mercifully forgive us in all our sins. Amen.

II

"I will miss you, Blanche, honestly," Victor tells me softly. So softly that his words seem like a silent dream. I'm very quiet, sitting down. "I'm tired of de Boere doctors telling me 'we'll make sure you'll come out of here a Nationalist, 'Yes baas, no baas, thats right baas.' I had to lie to them and say that I was feeling better. Fok them, man! The filthy swine! We can never look them into their eyes. But they fear us all, slaves, all of us–mental slaves. Their policy is oorvat en afvat (conquer and take). The Boer try to break our spirit. It will be our day, one day, *our* century. To leave, to forget, that's what I must do now. Better that to face than the constant electric shocks they force on us blacks. Things will come right for you, you'll see. Ag man, it's not so bad here. And I'll write to you. I promise I will."

"There's nothing left here for me Victor. Maybe just my sister's family. But it feels like a wasteland where all that has been is lost. So many times people have left me, all whom I loved. My husband. My children. The country is in a state of chaos, madness. Let's not talk of love letters. There's no time, and I must return to my journal writing. Go well, Victor. Thank you. Don't post me anything. It will only make things more difficult..."

"Come now–you don't mean that, Blanche. I'll write to you whether you want to or not."

"Go fight for and find...your blerrie Azania!"

He comes my way to put his arms around me, as if it is the last time we will ever see each other. But I throw him off me, only my hand touches his hand. Hands, not hugs, tell our fate.

"You know, Black Consciousness is just important in fighting for women, I think, as it is about liberating black people." He reaches out again, quickly hugs me tightly in the corner of an out-of-the-way place, and looks deeply into my weary eyes. So deep that my heart sinks. Eyes that have known more pain than most.

"I'll never forget you."

"Will you remain in the country?", I ask him.

"I don't know. So many of us are leaving with nothing but the shirts on our backs. Our lives are controlled by paper passes. Maybe I'll keep wandering. Stop speaking Afrikaans. And you?"

"Can I ever escape here, escape from my demons? My dream is to be with my children. That is my only dream, over and over again. That is any mother's dream."

Smiling, he takes hold of my bronzed hand. "I'll send you some of my newspaper columns..."

Victor walks to his daughter's motor-car, looking back one more time at me. He waves, and says words I vaguely remember he taught to me during our many months here. I don't wave back, but stand there at the towering iron gate of the sanitorium, watching as they motor away in the distance. Alone, watching my secret confidant and life go away from me, again. I had hoped that maybe it would be Victor driving that motor-car with me in it. Never to return to this place again, never again to come back to South Africa. But maybe it was all a delirious dream–a coloured woman and an African. The constant threat of being called a kaffir-lover, of being sent to prison. But this time it wasn't a married white man with a poor coloured hoer. Many minutes pass before I can move from where I stand. I close my eyes, and take a deep, deep breath. My mind blankens with thoughts of death. The wind sandpapers me: the heat is so blistering that I should hide from it but do not. Tears mix with sand. Adoration begins to fade, and I do not wipe my eyes. The sun quickly dries them. I dream of another place. Dream of my children, seeing them grow up and get married, and of me watching over my grandchildren.

III

That night Blanche dashed out into the darkness and furiously attacked whomever she encountered, just like Soera Brotto, a slave who had killed seven people and ran amok in the streets of Cape Town in 1786. Only men aroused her fury. Maybe she swung her frail fists at large frightening trees in the dark. She couldn't remember. It was all a terrific nightmare. She was found a day later, hungry, fatigued, wimpering with white clay on her face–her slight body heaving like a small wounded animal and sighing in the still silence about her. No one was there to comfort her, to save herself, from dying deep. Deep inside.

She stopped eating for a time, which seemed forever. The straightjacket of apartheid wrapped around her agonizingly. The anguish of being robbed of her friend and suitor brought back the pain of losing her husband and children nearly ten years ago. It nearly broke her. Her hands shook as she took her tablets with water to help her sleep. "Blanche, the students are rioting in Soweto, the schools are burning and the army is killing them," said a sister to her. But she did not respond. Many times she lay awake, listening to the scream of the sonbesie, the sun beetles, her mind numb, her eyes not leaving the horizon as it descended from the small corner of the window in the ward. Pen and paper were taken away from her as punishment, although she could request her prayer book. She was not permitted to wear panties and even cotton wool was not given to her to stop her menstrual flow. She felt that she could not go on; demons plagued her once again. Life seemed as barren and manic as in Namqualand, with its hot, brick-red soil, scattered with endless dunes and awash in the exploding colour of wondrous flowers. She thought of her many months with Victor, sharing the newspaper, talking and walking alone but together, as if they were not really in a mental hospital, but in an intoxicating place somewhere else, not even in South Africa, but somewhere–anywhere, free. It was hard for her to leave her bed, and the sisters knew that something significant had led to a relapse in her melancholy. It was as if she really wasn't living, but perishing inside. And she could tell no one, the sisters, not even one of her confidants, what had magically transpired between herself and her journalist-friend.

As Christmas approached she did not want to eat the usual biscuits that came with meals. She slept restlessly again, and dreamed that she was being decapitated. She was always running in her nightmare or sitting with other women at a fire, chanting, trance-like, as her movement intensified, with piercing cries in the distance–a call for help–and the same image appearing, that of the horned eland, a healer and rain-bringer. Hands were put on her naked body, on her chest and back, as if to draw out the evil humour and transfer healing energy through hot sweat. "Kai! Kai! Kai!" she heard the !Khung medicine dancers wail, their caped bodies silhouetted by the dawn as her sickness was thrown out of her exausted and feverish body. The haze of the moon's mist was upon them, with the high dune hills and mongono nut trees in the back. It cast a shadow on all, it's light looking at them as they moved majestically, rhythmically, in a dance that she had seen as a child somewhere. They danced so fiercefully that the circle on the sandy ground became a noticeable groove ditch, running up to their calves. She felt as though she were alone, but a radiant warmth soon overcame her. People knew her not by her first name, but by another, which she had never mouthed before.

A silent hum was heard above the pitchdark sky and in that hum she came to feel a soothing voice: "Que soy era Immaculada Councepciou." Was it Ma? Or just another demon? All time stopped as the full moon stood still in the night's sky. She now looked at things–the world–upside down. And the light shone on her naked body, touching her softly, glowingly, for all to see. A bright orangy white flame. Then she heard another voice: "The name of my place is called home..." Yet she did not understand its meaning. She felt as if she were running, heart pounding. She could hear her hard breath, see it in front of her in the blue-green mist. The sound of water, dripping, trickling in the cool distance. Her body and the palms of her hands were wet with perspiration.

A sudden calm overcame her for some unknown reason. And now a Christ-like figure, an image, appeared before her. Its voice was that of a woman, and it looked like a black man, hands extending towards her, towards her. Eyes up, comforting her. Like the son whom she had given birth to. Silence. Soft still silence. Her breathing steadied. Heart nearly stopped. She was given a cup of water. She sipped its coolness. And as she looked up, the gigantic golden moon was again upon her, its light casting a shadow on all, and the night beat on. A mirage was seen in the distance. A blue mist like smoke that filled her lungs. Then, sleep, sleep, precious sleep...

She awoke in the middle of the night, sweating, as if it were full summer. Maybe a spirit had come to her. Blanche could only lay there softly and silently, her thoughts still racing, the sound of her heartbeat pounding as loud as the crickets chirped outside. How to stop this incessant pounding in her heart and her quick and endless thoughts, she did not know.

Slowly, very slowly, she resumed some of her activities. Jams were prepared and sold by the boarders of the hospital to people in Benoni. The swift fingerwork of the women in gently squeezing, smoothing, and shaping coils of clay to create solid pots was something that brought joy to her. Comfort. The women would carefully examine each pot for cracks, and if there were none, they would be prepared for firing, then cooling. And in between there was time to speak about the day, even of her thoughts of her children. It was as if the feel of the finished pots brought the touch and feel of her children closer to her, from overseas. As Christmas approached, she decorated cards. She pasted delicate yellow and purple petals from flowers that grew on the grounds of the hospital on the covers of each. In one of the hand-made greeting cards, she wrote in a stylized hand that seemed a bit shaky: "Wishing you a very happy Christmas and prosperous New Year." This was sent to Katherine who was now approaching eighteen. Blanche's letters or cards did not say much, save for if she became worried if her eldest daughter stopped writing to her, or if she desperately needed money for winter clothing. Sometimes there would be a ten rand note enclosed in a birthday card, or a final sentence to Katherine and the others reminding them to "look after yourselves and be obedient."

***

I had arrived unexpectedly to bury my mother on a weekend at the end of November in 1996 in Gauteng, the place that was once called the Witswatersrand during the days of apartheid and prior to this. The new name was the Sesotho name meaning "Place of Gold," and it showed how South Africa had changed once democracy was rapidly underway. The old, cranky Afrikaner airport customs officials had been replaced by smiling Africans.

People were humming to the tune of "White Christmas" at the airport when I arrived, finally. How strange, as it was summer-hot outside as I greeted my waiting relatives all in shorts and cotton tops. I was quickly transported to my aunt's small house in Riverlea, a coloured area.

"She cried and cried for you people each day, after you left in 1969," my uncle said to me. "I don't think she realized what she did when she signed the papers to give you your freedom, to give you to your father when he decided to go to Canada," he went on to tell me as he quivered, taking his cup of tea from the small table next to the tattered couch we were both sitting on. He coughed away terribly. "Your grandfather once told your father...not to treat your mother like an animal after she ran away back home with you four children to stay with us after your father mistreated her so." I remained silent, feeling that, as my father's only son, I was implicated in this somehow.

Later, after hugs and hellos, I settled down a bit and came into the living room. The television blared as we watched another American rerun on SABC 1. My mind raced with a terrible sadness that only a child could know. I was angry no more, just grief-stricken and deep within myself. All that I could think was of my only trip to see her ten years back. A friend had told me to see her soon, two years prior to her death. But I had not. I couldn't afford to and part of me had been afraid of seeing her, I suppose. Afraid of knowing that she was on death's door, that the misery she faced was continuing over and over again. For her and for us. And even as we telephoned her off and on, she remained silent, silent as an unforgiving ghost on the other side.

i, moffie

April 15, 1986, just outside a Sanitorium, Republic of South Africa

In the distance the African sun was setting. A luminous orange glow hovered across the expanding horizon, a single line of the flat country is drawn and this place is the moment I've wanted to touch, see, feel. No matter what the consequences. The fiery descending ball would later disappear into a cloudless wide sky, and be replaced by a bright moon that spoke to us.

Somehow things seemed so new, so unreal, and reminded me that I was now in my native South Africa, not Canada. I was, indeed, *home*. In the back of an automobile, I was holding my mother silently, close to me, waiting for my auntie's return, waiting to see if we could get an extension on my mother's weekly pass from this place she knew as home. What horrors existed here, I could only imagine. As a father would a child, I held my mother tightly, caressing her straggly grey hair, the roles reversed this time for a son and his mother.

"Did I ever tell you...about Francis? His words changed me." Complete silence from her. I didn't think that she had understood, but I was glad that we were together, finally. Then again, in the condition she was in, my question would require many minutes for her to verbalize a coherent response. To think that for seventeen years these long minutes together were what I had hoped for, wished for eternally. My boyhood, teenhood and manhood all wrapped into one; my real life now thrust upon me, finally.

"Everything will be alright. Everything will be alright," I whispered to her gently, taking her wrinkled hand, holding it tight.

We stayed like this for what seemed an eternity. I peered outside of the parked white Rover. A shadow of darkness now fully covered the barrack-like hospital. The car, turned off. I took my free arm and continued stroking her hair. Calming her. Assuring her that I was now *with* her. One was either out or in, I thought. Diagnosed mad or sane. Sick or fit. Banned or free. I knew very little of my mother's life here. From what I could tell, she did not like this place. Would it be the death of her, I wondered? Would she ever escape this detainee's hell and find freedom? There was only one white psychiatrist who visited monthly. A large tree overlooked us.

"Did I tell you, Norman," she slowly breathed to me, "years ago, there was this one time, I was assaulted by a man. No," she mumbled. "*Raped...*" I sensed the pain in her body, in her hair that my palm brushed over, and I held her even more closely. So closely that I didn't want to ever let go of her again. I wished I could have been here to protect her. I would have castrated the man who did it... So many horrible things for her and us to withstand. No one here really to comfort her, to listen to her stories of loss, pain and brutality. Men's rage. Violence. Apartheid.

Why have I come to see her only now? Why did we not really know the truth of her existence, lost to the asylum? In being with her, I took on her name and asked for absolution.

12

praise poem for my moeder

and there i was
staring at your rose-petalled coffin
in the heart of the earth that gave life to you
Africa
Mummy
Mosadi
in the heart of (our) home
how could i forget you, how could i?
after all of the days, years, decades, mournful tears
after all of the endless telephone calls, letters, urgencies
when you cried silently inside and could not speak
and we died silently and could only listen
to your brave heart
and endless yearning sadness
for it was ours too, for it was our destiny too
and now that i have looked
at all of your forgotten photographs
and keepsakes, and our letters with freshly tears sprinkled all over them,
even the paper-covered prayer book
you so earnestly read, cried to, in your wakeful sleep
and now that i have realized that my whole life
was a deathful existence, so deathful that i needed
to hurriedly fly to bury you, to throw red curried earth
in your shallow grave, with no marker but my tides of tears
your frail yet brave coloured body
i held it in my frail, shaking hands
your african fires now silent, surrendered
your heart now a star aglow in the ocean-wide sky
all of us singing hymns as red-eyed attendants, sons of shaka, in indigo blue overalls,
they, our unacknowledged brothers, quietly lowering you into the ground,
your feet pointing downriver
as teardrops of rain fall to quench our bleeding thirsty hearts
i have realized this: our undying love could not be forgotten
to forget was to forget you
to forget was to forget south africa, azania too
to forget was to lose all hope
but to remember was to tell, to speak your name, to live
je me souviens de toi, maman
je me souviens de toi, maman

mothering my self

There is an unknown stillness about this distant place, and some voices from the trees
with the wind rushing through their leaves that say a million things more important
about life than city life. I am moving a bit easier, but feel like I am sixty, and the
pain from the stainless steel sutures after my hernia operation–fleshy tissue knit over
fleshy tissue, reminds me of her enduring anguish. Mummy's life. Frank, who lifted
my spirits, cycled here in the hot sun today and brought a fresh fruit and cheese
basket. Sweat dripped all over his clothes as he smiled at me at the front door of the
hospital. As we sat outside on a bench near the many planted flowers now in their
peak season, I heard that the gossip of the library was as funny as ever, and I begged
him not to make me laugh as I held my side fast. I still remember him saying: "Oh,
we're just bachelors," and then there was some more giggling–and pain as I buckled
over.

"Listen," he said, "promise me, if I tell you something will you promise not to
tell?"

"Okay, okay darling, tell me *everything*!" I pleaded hushingly.

And so began one of his usual funny stories as only a son of the Prairies could tell
it, of whom had done what at work–not by the book–and which library manager was
now rumoured to be on the dreary edge of work. Life never changes; bureacracies
silence and impale people.

Then he went on again: "Oh, but a friend came over Sunday night. And I scented
my best sheets and pillowcases. It must have been the vanilla-flavoured scent.
Yes...yes."

"Uh-huh," I said, tasting one of the fresh sweet peaches he had brought me.

Raising his eyebrows and turning his head this way and that, he whispered to me:
"Well *nothing* happened! He was just a sleaze-bag anyway!"

I couldn't stop with my laughing, bending over again from the immense abdomi-
nal pain, and telling him that his jokes were nearly "killing" me.

We soon settled down, then took a slow, slow stroll on the grounds afterward.
There was tea at that small beautiful waterfall with the sun on us and then he cycled
back home.

At age five, I had my first surgery in the hospital. My tonsils came out and my
parents came to see me. I cannot see their faces, but there is a strong and eduring
sense of them. This morning, I feel like that helpless child wanting to see his moeder
again. Her life-long absence and recent death are still among my thoughts, especially
each day as I walk slowly, slowly, on the fresh green grounds, breathing new life into
me. So things in life had finally caught up to me. Touching leaves, their breath still
alive, saying that their time to change into bright oranges and golden yellows was
nearly here. Everything–the wind, the trees, that I couldn't see or hear–spoke to me.
And I came to understand their meaning...

Does this place that feels like hallowed ground remind me of Mummy's cold sanitorium? Could it possibly be the same? Did she see us in the many companions she
spoke to, cried to, in the middle of the night? It is unthinkable that my convalescence
would be hers, that my brief but timeless four-day stay here at this estate-like hospi-

tal, its grounds neatly manicured with flowers exploding all around, with even deer running freely, could create her wrenching world. The asylum is not this place, and this place is not the asylum. There are no walls to climb over, escape from...

As the surgeon placed the sharp scalpel deep into my tense open groin, the white curtain hanging vertically to my chest hiding all (Jim Greeves was playing overhead–how eerie!), I tried to think of Mummy and her indomitable spirit, with me as I swam–stroking, slicing fast through miles of rough oceans–the unknown current becoming more furious as the shiny knife dug deep, deep, deeper. The drugs soon wore off, and the hard tugging of my skin felt strange, uncomfortable and disturbingly painful. "Doctor is everything fine?" I kept asking. More quick deep breaths puffing out from me, and the nurse keeps taking my pulse. And finally, all that I remembered was a quick hand-shake from my surgeon–like a sudden snapshot. Wheelchair-bound, I was whisked away to my room to lie down.

Maybe the penetrating, unending pain of surgery–like that of a knife still stuck into your flesh (as deep as the primal wound)–and the social isolation away from the comforts of home might remind me a bit of Mummy's torment. At mid-life I am a flower only beginning to heal.

One wants to escape to the outdoors, to breathe, to walk slower. Mummy, what do you see or hear, né? The joyful sound of us playing in our dusty backyard with Bonzo, our dog? The time I was scolded severely by Daddy for nearly burning down half of the house on Aster Road? The smell of burning hot toast and melting butter from your hot oven, which has never left me? The scent of me as a newborn as I was snub-nozed against your warm nipple while you gently sang and talked to me? Or the time when our kindly maid ran home terrified to her black location because she had forgotten her pass? Now that was the evil of apartheid speaking. That harrowing world still shackles us.

The look of those four towering trees are maybe what Mummy saw as they grew along with her, her spirit nearly broken but healing, that lonely woman who weeped, the breast that heaved. The long torture of losing not just one or two of her younsters–her children, her hope–but *all* four of them, and never to realize her own escape to freedom.

My strokes of tears are my mother's tears are my sisters' tears...

coloured days

district six
same as africville
bull-dozed–flat
where we lived, laughed and died
where our ancestors sang
songs to their children
too many memories
destroyed, erased
new governments
won't own up to the
loss of families living and loving there

my eighty-six-year-old uncle wants to
go back to the old country
to rightfully reclaim his piece of land
that was stolen from him, us
given to whites
at half the price, half the price
but whose land is it anyway?
for one cannot devour the earth

we had to go through the back door
of those people's homes
says he, rather bitterly
says he, rather bitterly

even helped poor whites
read and learn
watching them
take jobs away from us
our lives gone
the government claiming a white republic
couldn't live: read, laugh, swim, eat, even shit with them
damn finger-waving boers!
damn finger-waving boers!
vorster and botha were really our fathers
says my uncle bluntly

the coloureds were their blue-eyed sons and blond-haired daughters
but they refused to acknowledge it
the blaady boers laughed, calling us hotnots
huh–if only i could write the history of south africa
and the slave trade, too
that would truly be the day!

coloured days, coloured days
they come back to you
in so many different ways

like the time
i left the airport in jo'burg
to find thirty relatives
waving good-bye
all of us
looking the same
skins textured slightly, differently
but how alike i felt
photograph after photograph for keepsake
my country, my hopes all lost and found now
mummy, daddy too

and like the time i saw pictures of mummy
everywhere   dreaming of her
everywhere in sunny sad south africa

and like the time
i read about our ancestors
autoposies in the nineteenth century
focussed on hottentot and bushman females
sexual parts   sexual parts   their so-called apron made them
more susceptible to certain abnormal excesses   the love of another woman
ag man, the hottentot venus
her bones and genitalia–our history, our herstory
rests uneasily   uneasily
in european museums
in their places of idle gossip and giggles

coloured days, coloured days
they come back to you
in so many different ways

the moffee, ms. denise darcelle
parading, skirt up, bronzed skin, smiling with the dressed-up coons
just call me madame, bellows she, dancingly
at the cape carnival
something that delighted me
that was me, that would have been me

the way in which we were named as
children–stupid
lazy, drunken, dependant, chained
like blacks the world over

like slaves the world over

coloured days, coloured days
they come back to you
in so many different ways

growing up in the ice-cold of winter
remembering the warmth of the land
coloured cousins photographed–are they naaiing?
living, escaping to riverlea, eldorado's park, bosmont and newclare
golden cape gooseberry jam
bessie head–gone to live in botswana
everything, everything

mummy finally waiting for me/us
daddy wishing to forget her, yet unable to forget his days as a c.o.
forgetting the smell of police dogs tearing angry black flesh
my sisters, seeing traces of them in me, her
exiled, forgotten
as if time stood still
as if time shouted at me
remember, remember

coloured days, coloured days
they come back to you
in so many different ways

as if each yesterday were buried somewhere
in some faded memory, too distant to remember
as if each today were living in the thoughts of
my uncle and aunt in some far away place
sitting, waiting for a book–any word–to come out
about their disrupted and uprooted lives
what could have been
what should have been   coloured days

your face

the barrenness of your stark face
lined by rivers of sorrow, our bodies exhausted by their flow
told me something of my own life–of all of our lives
for grief was our only home
silent and threatening
and there was little to rejoice
each christmas
with cheap candies and nuts broken
by that old iron nutcracker oupa had used
the deathly silence nearly lifting

the gift of laughter and joyfulness
were not close cousins to us
nor were they present in our
everyday experiences
for her absence
was our ongoing death and life
all rolled into one.

Daddy

the blue-jeaned boy in baseball cap
sits patiently on the subway as its snakes away
in the deep dark tunnel
his leg sways from the ground as he waits to get off
his tired father remains next to him
hands dirtied by dust, hardened by life
the young child reminds me of my own father
who was as fond of children as i
but i cannot see our sheltered brown faces
bodies, gestures, senses, understandings, dark doorways
i can only fear his harsh words
feel anger at his brutal impatience
grow silent at our century
of longing–even forgetting–the alluring woman
whom we both loved, yearned for   but were lost to

the place we come from

"As youngsters, we looked after your father as a young charge showing him off," he recollected, "even catching hares and tortoises and climbing the mimosa thorn trees with him in Beaconsfield. One day on an excursion he left our attention briefly, and man did we ever receive a hiding from our father for it!"

Daddy liked to listen to the fairy stories of his older siblings, how he had excelled in reading, arithmetic and general knowledge and by the age of eight had already read three dozen books at primary school. At sixteen, he left high school, much to his family's dismay. "I thought that maybe he should attend medical school at the University of Cape Town, but your father had made himself older by one year and enlisted secretly in the Union Defence Force (UDF), serving later in North Africa as a member of the eighth army," I heard from the family's friend, Mr. James.

As a rising sargeant, my father did not like the ruling of the UDF that stipulated that a non-white soldier could never succeed to the status of Commissioned Officer, reserved only for white soldiers. Armed with only a bicycle and a monthly stipend of seventeen pounds, he returned to Kimberley upon discharge. He worked at the whole-sale firm of Awerbuck and Brown in Transvaal Road, and living at home, he helped his parents, assisting his father's meagre income as a garbage-truck driver. Later, he and another ex-serviceman Sonny Leon–who would later lead the Labour Party (visiting my father and us in 1972 to get support from the Canadian government and the West for sanctions against the apartheid government). Both had helped to register coloured voters in the rural districts "by the dozens," travelling throughout the Northern Cape from Vryburg to Upington, eventually helping Harry Oppenheimer win the parliamentary constituency of Kimberley, since the coloured vote would ultimately decide who won.

As a highly respected Commissioner of Oaths after Oppenheimer helped him and Leon in their appointments, my father was instrumental in applying for old aged people to collect their pensions. "Your grandfather, and other coloureds probably felt they weren't entitled to these," said the man I talked to, "so your father had an essential job to do. It was no easy task!" Here was a man who was highly regarded in the community, yet, as a family man, he would always have incredible difficulty. Yet his memories were fond of playing hockey with his chums in Newton, or of going to Modder River just outside of Kimberley for picnics on New Year's Day. It was after a hockey tournament at Hotel Kemo in 1954 when he would finally meet my mother after a match between the Transvaal Women's Hockey Team and the Griqualand West squad. Their young eyes must have sparkled so. Over the course of courting her for a year by travelling to Johannesburg where she lived with her parents, he married her despite having dated another woman earlier. He briefly mentioned that my father had not known about my mother having been in a mental hospital when she was an adolescent. But Mummy was alright for many years despite having given birth to four healthy children.

Then I heard something of slaves in the Cape and their importance. "I should also tell you about the great Malay doctor of Cape Town, Dr. Abdullah Abduraham. I must have been only twelve."

"Who was he?"

"His grandparents were well-respected slaves, and the African Peoples' Organization held its conference in Beaconsfield, Kimberley. My father was the secretary, and Mr. Abrahams the fishmonger was the Chairman of the Beaconsfield branch of the APO. Dr. Abduraham was the grand president who came to speak to the coloured people and the APO conference members."

"So what happened?" I asked inquisitively.

"After the conference, my father invited Dr. Abduraham to come over for tea. I was outside and my father introduced me to him. Dr. Abduraham then asked if I was still at school. 'Yes, doctor,' I replied.

"'How do you like school?' he asked me. I said, 'Oh, I love school, but my father keeps me from going early because I have to take his breakfast away.' My father was telling him that I wrote out the notices for the meetings each Tuesday monthly. 'Oh,' he said, 'One day you are going to take your father's place!' And I said, 'Yes, doctor.' 'Stay in school as long as you can. You'll never regret it!' he said. Then I was shooed out by my father to play with my chums."

There was another story of how Prime Minister Hertzog came and members of the APO went to hear him speak. It was December and extremely hot. "What about the coloured people–the bruin mense?" someone in the audience asked him. He said, "They are part of the white people of South Africa. We must never forget that because they speak our language–Afrikaans." The Afrikaners spoke Nederlands, and, in fact, coloured people, in Cape Town spoke more Afrikaans. "People made fun of you if you spoke English," I was reminded.

Apparently there were no white women when the first Dutchman, Jan van Riebeeck, arrived in South Africa. "Oh, only about eighty-one trekkers altogether, and that was 1852. He brought with them six women. There were many more coloured–Khoi Khoi and Hottentot women. The beachmongers," I was told. "That's where we got our coloured blood from. But the Afrikaners won't admit it today. They say 'no–we were mixed with Bushmen and Hottentots.' This is not true. The Boer–he'll make a wife of a servant girl and she'll bear him children and she will be dismissed from the farm. Those children are coloured–blue-eyed, golden-haired. That's a fact. They talk about the history of South Africa, man. Nonsense!" Mr. James, went on. But then again it seemed as though coloureds were too quick to lose sight of their African roots.

Over our delightful conversation, I learned that the flat-bottom steel pot, in which one put potatoes, rice and meat–that was one's potjie pot. "The Dutchmen claim that they were the originators of it. Not so. The African people, they were the true origina-tors of it. They would steam the rice on top and steam the food. They'd eat it all up." People assembled at Beaconsfield Townhall in 1925, I heard. "The ANC got their members away very carefully. The APO–there were Africans and Indians in it, and coloureds, too." But the ANC came to Kimberley for a conference and the family's friend was only a youngster of twelve. There were ousies, old women making food for the delegates.

"I jumped over the fence with a close friend," he went on.

"'Molo umfana' one lady said.

"'Molo mamma,' I said respectfully.

"'Can we help you?' we said.

"'Oh, what can you do?'

"'We can chop the wood!'

"'Oh, yes, bring some wood,' we were told.

"A fire was made, and we were waiting until the food was cooked on a true potjie pot.

"'You'll get your share now,' she said to us.

"Then we waited another blaady half hour and then she dished up our meal on a tin plate. We got some rice, then a bit of vegetables, and finally a very small piece of meat, jong!

"'Come and sit in the corner,' I said to my pal. We were blaady hungry man. These people, the African women were very kind. Man, those were the days!"

"People used to powder themselves white," I heard later over tea. He continued again, "They'd want to be on the white side. Some couldn't play white because they were dark. One of the darkest would powder herself really white."

I asked him if a lot of coloureds were doing this.

"Oh, yes! Not only *playing* white, but going over to the white side! The wages were tops for whites. They lived in the best houses and better areas. That was the big thing on people's minds."

"Was it economics then, not really politics?"

"I suppose so. But some people were nasty about it. A few relatives were fair-skinned. But they were very nice to us. Frankie went to join the airforce overseas during the war. They were all on the white side. They went over to them, and didn't just *play* white."

In Canada, this man, a close family friend, took the place of a Basotho storyteller–a keeper of the family's stories. Like an elder African griot or town crier or spiritual messenger, he weaved his tales as if they had just occurred, bringing meaning to the good and bad of life. Kimberley was also famous for nick-names: a man he knew there would be called ou dikkop because he had a thick head. "When I got to the mudhouse in Beaconsfield to say a few words at his funeral, I didn't even know the man's real name until then!" We shared a laugh. Another would be called a name in Afrikaans because his bum stuck out, or because he had wagonwheel ears, or another–his lip was swollen after a spider had bitten him there and it "stood out like a big sausage," he roared.

"Oh, yes, we had special names for the whites. Jong, they had rude names and I don't want to repeat them," his wife who joined us, added laughingly. Her flame was flickering, not as bright now, but she was as gentle as Mummy, smiling. Making fun was the only way for coloureds to fight back–through satire and prodding fun at their exploiters. Coloureds had little control over their lives in which whites dictated. They had to be funny–snaaks, buffoons–in order to keep sane because of the cruelty of apartheid. It was a "purifying device, an escape valve, an outlet for [generations] of feelings of frustration, hatred and hostility," wrote Vernon A. February, finally.

Dearest Mummy

May 1, 1971

How are you doing? I hope fine. We haven't heard from you for quite a while now. Did you receive our letter, posted a few weeks ago? I have great news to tell you. I am getting confirmed tomorrow. I wish you were here to see me do this. I have a lovely pair of white shoes and stockings, and I am going to buy my new dress this afternoon. Mrs. Jacobs is going to do my hair, and it's going to be in curls, like a bun. We had to practise how to walk up and down the aisle, and where to sit, etc. We don't have to wear white veils. Last Friday, April 23-24, we went to this camp, called Camp Artaban. We had a lovely time there. We went to the confirmation group. They are very friendly, and nice to have as friends. Tell Aunty Violet and Aunty Filda that I am getting confirmed because they are my godmothers. Daddy gave me all of the money for my confirmation clothes and money for the camp, too. We have a very nice minister, Rev. Clarke. We had two ladies helping us with the confirmation. They are very nice people, too.

I have enjoyed the confirmation because I met many new friends and really what this whole confirmation course was about was to grow closer to each other and to know them better. Now we are full members of the Christian church. And on May 16th, we are going to have our First Holy Communion and on that Sunday we are supposed to come as families to the service. May 9th is going to be Initiation Sunday and that means we are supposed to come to the church on Sunday evenings because it's a youth group. And on the last Sunday in May we are going to have a Pot Luck Supper. Each one brings either a salad or dessert or something else.

Regards to all. We miss you.

Your loving daughter,

Katherine

she moved

she moved
in between smouldering cigarettes
and deep, deep sighs, unable to breath
her nearly always sad, contemplative look at him
she, wanting mummy–always
old faded report cards
you know–the ones from standard seven
that said she got straight A's
the photo of her as a smiling baby in knitted new pink clothing mummy made
the first child, the girl will always be close to mummy, even closer to daddy
then there was her fading baptism card she still kept–she read the prayer on it always
and wanted to smile but couldn't, always tears, always unknown fear
she tried to remember the church–all saints in beaconsfield, where the cool water made
her cry
the smiling photo of mummy, looking like a fashion model, cooldrink and cream cake
at the table
the photo of the eldest as head prefect at transvaal road primary school
she in two long, long braids, glasses on, perfectly pinning something on a smiling
basil d'oliveira
the famous coloured cricketer, who left the republic for england because the government
only wanted whites to play by themselves, like coloureds and blacks, separated

then there were her women's monthly magazines
old and cheap, that she couldn't decide
whether or not to keep
as garbage or adornments
to her tiny one-room place
which she had to share with
a mental patient who was still
in the hospital, who tried to strangle her in her sleep
and many times later, her hands shaking, shaking
he'd listen, his heart weeping
to her stories of blackened bananas
and watered-down milk
of blackened bananas
and watered-down milk
while she ran out each night, left with only enough to buy a sour coffee and smoke-filled
donut
the photo of her in the 70s to her time with her brown bubbly baby of
bathing her in the small sink of the government house where they lived,
daddy saying don't have too many canadian friends
splashing, splashing, smiles, smiles
the child was born in that hospital; the father died there, and they four heard mummy's
soft, funny and frightening voice there
the marriage's happier days...that child brought such joy–love to their impoverished

lives, he said
but even then, she cried to her ex-husband's mother that she couldn't marry the man
this on her wedding day, as her white dress dripped with bloody tears
there won't be any kaffir-lovers in my house, daddy said long before
there won't be any kaffir-lovers in my house, daddy said long before
and now he was there, in that snap, standing proudly with her, the eldest in island's sun
she the mother of the children who knew no mother but her
she the child who knew no mother but her
after that long, long flight
leaving mummy, leaving mummy, when would she see her again?

old crinkly papers from daddy's death
which she had kept
he folded them neatly, slowly
as any good son would do now
even though he hadn't forgotten his anger at the old man
or his deathly drinking

she moved
only to find that
there was nothing left of her things
that gave her life any meaning
not even the worn curry-stained recipe books of
special dishes that she loved making, that reminded her of mummy again–her things,
pots and dishes
before she ran to the shelter, after he bruised and cussed her for the last time
even the fashionable brown redwood shoes
which she bought but couldn't afford did not cheer her

he moved
her things into garbage bags, doubled, ten of them
as storage for his place
the guilt the brother felt as he told her his home was
too small, but where was she, his motherly sister to go but there?
that boarding house not fit for human beings
the night was cold and dark and spoke of unknown things
and he hoped he had the energy to console her and the other one, still

she moved going upscale now to high park
on one hundred and sixty three dollars a month
that's what the government called
comfort allowance, bless them, FUCK them the white bastards!
as if it allowed one to *live* comfortably
as if it helped people to feel less down
as if it helped people to live   better lives
she moved

queen street salad

and so we met again, greasy greek $2.99 salad
damp lettuce leaves, sprinkled sadly with her tears
she ate it as if it were her last meal
pushing down fries, washing down water, drinking coke all at once
sit up, grace, sit up!
eyes come to meet mine, she raises her back, slowly like an old woman
lipstick smeared, her last bit of "femininity" left
the police in new york gave me back my seventy dollars to take a bus home, she said
you've had a tough life, i answered back
uh-uh–fun!
but she forgot about the many keys to hotels in men's rooms that we found amongst her things
yet remembered the happy wedding of the second she was never invited to   more tears
and she could not jump the high fence to leave this place, asylum, madhouse
with floors which smelled of linoleum, with dirtied grimy toilets and rooms for the
walking dead
this lonely, lonely white ward where unshaven forgotten
men spoke in quick tongues, tongues that did not caress but made her laugh and cry stupidly
now smiles at me, hands more steady, still hunched over her meal
like christ at his last supper with only one loved one in attendance
goes over next door to buy one   two   three cigarettes
and quickly comes back   the salad was good, she says politely to the silent owner
table manners that come only from living in a south african family
coughs deeply   coughs more deeply   like daddy before he died
no needle in her ass   no needle in her ass from the diabetes
stopped the nurses from queen street
i'm no stupid mental slave, she screams
as old white men, dressed unassuredly, drink the stale coffee that they will pay for
at the end of the week in this monotone café, like the rest of them on this street
her sleepy mascared eyes look drowsily at me
i may have to go on welfare, been on f.b.a. too long
how are you to survive, i ask   in a boarding home
and doesn't that scare you?   no, not really
i'm better looking than the eldest, want to see my pictures, want to see my pictures?
she applies make-up to her chocolate brown tired face
a face that has seen more life, more death than the rest of us
i have the snaps of mummy   her funeral, the beautiful casket   two years ago in south africa
bring them, next time, she says finally, but remember to lock your door, lock your door tonight...
we leave each other on queen street, its landscape slowing changing
she, in her too tight boots   the ones that don't lace up all the way on her size ten feet
wearing her crinkled long black leather coat she found somewhere
that some 70s chick fitted on yonge and picked up her first boyfriend in
i take the back seat on the streetcar where no one will see my tears splashing on my
blank pages

exile/life

his hard sea shell of life
was finally broken
only for it to mend
once
once
once
after leaving his
deathly home, his miserable father
thick smoke on bright orange drapes hanging
like bitter naartjies on dying trees
after leaving his
curried dishes eaten with mango chutney
his mattress
it, too   falling apart
like the listless life
that had never been
with her
without his mournful mother, meek from abandonment, herself
where was ma?   where was ma?
no more mealie meal mornings

for she was really him
for she was really his only desire
over and over again
until the sea crept up
to meet them both
to mend his stony shell
and open up the world
to him
to open up his will
to live, love, leave, learn

and so it came to pass
that i met you, both of us coloured
both of us lost to white things, ideas
and so it came to pass
that i let go of
every fucking thing
every fucking stain
on my bloodied shirt
bloodied by thirty years

of pain and loss
of isolation and misery
the silent sea can sweep clean
life
can sweep clean
my bloodied shirt
of life
my bloodied body
the bread
of christ
and let us speak of things
so terrible and beautiful
so painful and pleasurable
that only two of us
will know the silence
of our heartfelt voices
the sweet sound of swallows
sweeping above
the darkness soon fading overhead
us

the shirt

i am contentedly wearing daddy's striped canary and beige shirt today
the same one he liked to put on in the heat of the day
as sweat poured down, fingers, eyes touching the evening's news
my thin brown body was too afraid to shed clothes in front of him
the unfashionable pants and awful grey pointed suede shoes he bought for me are
still there
but now i wore his tattered white undershirt, his hot diamond miner's sweat is my
gym sweat
i *am the child of he who was he who was he*
yet forget the small silent notes we passed to each other
left strewn like unheard cries on the old brown bookshelf in the *living* room
where he ate on the food-stained t.v. guide, smoked, slept, snored, read, thought of
rugby, the boys, the mines, maggy, mummy

and the shirt shelters me, protects me
hanging loosely, softly, my lanky hairy arms
and body hold it up, straight up, high up, up, up
it is mine, treasured
like his tarnished africa service medal   the great war for *civilization*
rescued after i last saw his body lying there on that cold hospital bed
he'd always give away his clothes, things to chums, cousins, uncles–smilingly
silent noble gestures of love
like the gift-giving san

i am contentedly wearing daddy's striped canary and beige shirt today
the same one he liked to put on in the heat of the day
as sweat poured down, fingers, eyes touching the evening's news
my thin brown body was too afraid to shed its clothes in front of him
the unfashionable pants and awful grey pointed swede shoes he bought for me are
still there
but now i wore his tattered white undershirt, his hot diamond miner's sweat is my
gym sweat
i *am the child of he who was he who was he*
yet forget the small silent notes we passed to each other
left strewn like unheard cries on the old brown bookshelf in the *living* room
where he ate on the food-stained t.v. guide, smoked, slept, snored, read, thought of
rugby, the boys, the mines, maggy, mummy

narrative of sister januarie, 1826

master say he want me not work pickin, the house needs tendin, the baby needs my breas say masters wife; another vrije burgher needs slaves, the word of my people say. the husband, the husband works for him, and gives the master his shillings. the pourboire makes him a drunkard as he sleeps in the cattle kraal. it makes him not think of the children, me. i's told masters wife "no" to chores in the kitchen, and now i's to be flogged with rods.

i's to be taken to town, the sun pierces my eyes. even though i's heavy my clothin, de whippin, scars me, my shoulders and buttocks, too. i's still member de slicin slicin sound of de thick leather rods. de pain is like satan coming for you. i's never forget it. i's just nearly half dead, laying in de bunk two days while de children and de husband help me. gittin over dat whippin still scars me, in de heart and de head, till dis day. scars runnin like flamin deep swirlin rivers crossin my torn body...

five days later, after the meals have been cooked for all, i's go to the kitchen, and de fire comin from de stove warms my body. my tired hands wash his pale back as he hums as if life is beautiful. i's dream of swimmin, runnin away far, far, never to feel his beastly touch again.

word of our emancipation will come soon, and our ancestors await this day. our whistles to each other at nights end are silent; punishment is swift, but i's still can't sleep on my back.

slavery/work

chained
whipped
brutalized
with no life
of their/our own
working the fields/offices
all day
yes baas, no baas
losing wives, babies
the one shot
in the head
by that boer farmer
"not guilty, not political"
said the apartheid judge
losing lives, losing everything
losing time, losing creativity
to bureacracy
to middle-class worries
following the north star
following the stock markets
coming this way
this way
to escape
freedom
find it
must
find it
before
we get caught, burned, lost
before i get caught
in the modern-day slavery
work

the second sister

we never called
but when we spoke
the words ranged from sorrow to kindness
unknown silences, unknown silences we know too well

and now she, too has lost her
job
again
deeply downhearted, she says
at daycare, like the other, she adds
collecting UI close to christmas
just in time

can't really drive on busy highways–the cars
concentration is pretty bad right now, i hear

i gotta go, i gotta go
she whispers, i gotto go
after eleven minutes
after no word from her
for eleven months
partially my fault
telling her that
i never wanted to speak to her again
for two years

she had forgiven Him
she slowly says   in her own way   through christ, his way
and this after many months
while my story of Him was not
that kind

i'm taking care of the eldest, i mention
money   that's okay
we can't afford gifts
this year, she sighs

take care, keep busy i tell her
plan your day well

click

and in her story i came to know her finally

We were on my balcony drinking white South African wine–Blouberg, I think it was called and made in Stellenbosch, listening to the rhythmic pulse of mbaqanga music and also tasting Ceres fruit juice. As I sipped the sweet wine from my glass, I could imagine the black and even coloured farmhands who still worked the white-owned farms. And the poor ill-treatment they received. Meagre wages. Some might sleep in places unfit for animals, while the whites looked on, lashing out at them with their eyes, only wanting to see the day's work done, and the money in the bank.

The candlelight was drawn to her brown face, now much older. The years had brought us all together, since their death. An hour or so passed before we talked about the things that people might talk about intimately, closely.
"Ja, maybe I don't fit in–here. The gay community is not for me. And even though I define myself as being black, I still don't feel I belong to the black community," I said, eyes looking to the horizon.
"Oh...you're in between, then," she said.
"Still coloured after all of these years? Huh, I don't know. I'm not a child of this country, but feel like a stranger in a strange land."

The clouds in the distance became darker as the sun set, and we could see the lights from planes blinking in the sky overhead. We continued to share mouthfuls of grapes and sweet canteloupe, talking of the first and second, how their lives still mirrored Mummy's. Then she spoke, finally, leaving out the part that she sill hugged her self to sleep at night, since childhood.

"I couldn't look at Him in the eyes. I was terrified of Him. Don't you remember how all of us sat in that bland living room as kids, watching TV, maybe it was a comedy–*Sanford and Son*. We were on one end of that smoke-filled, tattered couch. And He was there, sitting in that old chair with his newspapers. But there was no word from any of us, even when there was a funny moment. And it was like we were all there but weren't. Dying not living. Quiet, so quiet we couldn't breathe."
I jumped in: "Could you imagine if something broke, how we would all react? Maybe as if nothing had happened, as if we were all dummies and just the television was speaking." A huge laugh came from me because it seemed so ridiculous now, like a tragic comedy that only a working-class South African family knew.

"It's like I've had this great inner strength because of the things that have happened to me, us. I had to go on," she started again. "I don't remember mourning for Him or Her when they finally passed away. Was I blocking out my feelings? Maybe I had to escape from the family to survive in the end. To keep whole. To keep sane. *The centre had to keep together.* Maybe when I left the husband, him, too, I had to be strong. And my minister asked me, 'What are you doing?' when I was briefly in that awful shelter. 'Working!' I said. And from that day on, I knew I could *live*, maybe somehow go on..."

coming/knowing

i jerk off to a made-up picture   fully coloured
flipping through a girlie magazine   the only one   i've had for five years
pages now missing moments of desire abandonned
a stiff cock rides close to the entrance of her desirous doorway
to the entrance of the world
what the world wants
what men want
what he still might want
probing
thinking
imagining
brown tan line still showing from hot black days
in my four-way mirror   four different reflections of me, staring at me
legs tensed against the bed, heaving up,   up,
                                        down
after a soapy steamed bath
after blowing out a candle
and making a wish for them
whispering to god for her, her and her
leather cock ring on as i quietly breathe out on my hard bed   .
leather cock ring on   more lube
faster, faster the tip only please
ja, that feels nice
as i look in the mirror of me
a shaven chest and muddy brown balls shaven, smooth
perineal desire pulsating
a thought of roy crosses my mind
david, mona
like all other lonely nights
nights when the howling wind
licks my body cold, shivering
as i walk from the gym unaccompanied and sing songs to myself
which my father hummed slowly to me
yet i do not hear the tears i take home with me   mummy   the rest
at thirty-seven
i'm past looking   only wanting
past knowing   only understanding
that life is
a bottomless murky mysterious lake
with me pulling myself
out, alone

and your kind hand wasn't there
wasn't there to help me out, drenched
even though i looked for it
my heart knew despair as if i were a child again
like every night i thought of you in 87, 92, 79
as the train shouted out on that tressle i eyed from
the dirty apartment window, my bare room contained little
it was as if i watched the world go by and no one asked me
where is your mother–*why*?
and the time i broke my arm in middle school
when daddy ran from his work picking up garbage
the strong smell still on his brown, hardworking hands
hands that knew misery, gave pain
hands that tried to mother
eyes worried, eyes worried
the pain of africa painted all over us

digging out

deep
deep, blankets of snow
as you plough through, hood up n' tight
after you just hugged your mug of coffee
bitter hot sweet mornings
your breath spitting out in front of you like a ghostly mist
feeling the cold wetness hitting your worn feet, knowing only hot sands
boots not laced up tightly
makes you think of loneliness, love
of still still sleepless death, paradise
you want to lie like an angel on the mile of fluff ahead of you
close your eyes, let snowflakes land all over you, kiss your ice-cold ebony cheeks
the veld's warmth is still hot in your mind, and so was *she*, all of them as puffy white
flakes fall down playfully, smiling, reminding you of childish dreams of longing for
home
pine trees bear white fluff heavy with emotion
listen to its silence
hear
it call out your lonely name
winds circling you
around you
asking you to
tread
your
blue path of life
through
its
thick white sea
red hot sun hitting you in the face
alone, thinking

paint me mon amour

your indigo blue kente cloth dance
the majestic sway of kings and queens
its rise and fall to the rhythm of a hypnotic drum beat
the one you did for me at mayaro beach
against my body, the cloth now taken off
coconut palm trees swaying in the warm breezy night
blue waves of exile washing us dry
when we were last together   wanting
feels like
the finespun weave
of my mother's
finest table cloth, the only one
that came to me unscarred on our long lost journey
from africa
south of the sahara
your deep chocolate-brown body
moved
on my yet unpainted canvas
your sweet-tasting delicate palm, thick calluses exposed to the brutal elements
brush stroking
soft, hard, soft, hard, caressing
sweetsweetsweet
like a principal dancer
eyes smiling
igniting his or her stage
romantic red acrylic paint left on the band of your
sweaty tight white underwear
for me only to notice, touch, smell
the letsoku you applied made our thin, young, boyish chests glimmer so
curtains lifting, stage lights dimmed
lips, legs, hands colliding
in wet rains that kiss us tenderly

new york, 1994

A lanky chestnut-brown man, many years past my age, caught my attention. He was sipping a tall glass of wine. As he was speaking with one of his friends, he briefly looked me over as I stood reading from various posters on the walls of the dimly lit small bar I had just entered.

"My, my, chile, you my kina man, pretty with straight hair!" he yelled to me hands on hips. The guy called me over to get a better look while I smiled at him, telling him my name.

"Girl, yaw accent says you from outta state. We New York girls *sure* know how to tell where a man's from. The way he walks, struts hisself, the way he poses and wears his things–clothes that are raging–not from the ghetto. Naw, I say–you *not* from here."

"I'm from Toronto," I told him, hoping that he wouldn't reject my company.

"Toronno! Hell chile, I know 'bout that Caribbean festival that the girls go to evry year there! It's island stuff, its music that affects my body and nappy hair. Now you girls sure know how ta throw a pardy!"

"Uh huh, that's Caribanna and it sure does attract lots of black brothers and sisters from here. It's in August. Civic holiday," I answered back. He kept looking me over like he wanted to lick me or something. My eyes caught his thick black eyeliner and the hand with painted nails that held his glass in a delicate manner.

"You can call me Shirlee, chile, he said to me," extending his soft hand. "My friends, theys all call me Shirlee. Same with the husband." I shook it and looked around to see who else was here. Keller's was the place where banjee boys came, and tonight men walked in and out, since it was so close to the piers where the celebrations would take place. Shirlee was dressed as a man tonight in big blue painter's pants. "That gold chain you wearin' sure is fierce," she told me as she reached to touch it. I blushed and told her that my first boyfriend had given it to me and that it was my first time in New York. Said she lived in the Brooklin for years. Without much thought I asked her if she was excited about Pride weekend. Our lengthy conversation led me to ask her about the piers.

"Chile them piers is our own tarred beach. Hell, honey we do *more* than gawk there."

I chuckled. "What's up with all of those signs posted over the fences there anyway? You know: WHO KILLED MARSHA P. JOHNSON?"

She was silent for awhile, taking a long, long sip from her glass, her fingers caressing it. Her eyes said it all. "Hell, she was a friend a mine. They wouldn't even let her march side 'em in the first march in '70. Naw they tell her she can't come walk in drag. But she tell the middle-class white queers that she gonna organize her own Gaywalk for Freedom." Retrieving a hankerchief from her purse to dab at her watery eyes and leave her mascara intact, she told me more of her story. "That poor girl who had the charm of Oprah and the body of Jordan...hell she was found floatin' like a fallen angel. Like a fallen angel in the Hudson! That girl wasn't in drag, girl–the last time people said they saw her. They found her incognegro, chile. No hair or make-up. Hell no, Miss Thing didn't want to go that way."

I asked the big bartender for a quick refill. He came over and told Shirl not to fret, giving her a drink on the house.

"This place is tired, chile," she said as she gulped down from her full glass. "I come to see the sunset. The children–they come here like they ain't no tomorrow. Marsha, she murdered even before gettin' anyplace. You know...the big dream. Big fuckin' American dream. All the girls here get caught up in dat shit. We still dying like flies, like fuckin' flies..."

There was a long, long silence and then finally, Donna Summer's "Last Dance" boomed. Drinks flowed. Brothers in the bar were now squeezing in here by the dozens, and I became claustrophobic, still thinking that beneath the joyous luster of gay life, misery and an unknown path persisted.

"Maybe some good will come out of this weekend," I said, trying to help ease my quick friend's pain. "Hell, maybe the cops will get new information on what happened to her." She looked up at me. Smiled. Her watery eyes looked down, slowly, then away from me, fading into the distance. I took another gulp of my watery beer and told her it was time for me to go.

Two round kisses on the cheek came from me, and I placed my arm on her shoulder. "Hope to see you at the UN."

"Honey, we plan to march ourselves 'cause they don't want us again. It's Miss Thang and them AIDS activists, and no one–no fuckin' cop, no mayor gonna say no to us. Don't you be doin' too much with the children now. Ya hear?"

"I won't..."

She glanced at me with her big brown eyes, waving so long. "I'm gonna try to work the obra, and see if my magic will help us New Yawk queens."

from here to district six

exile/d
from misery/life
his outcast mother rotting away
in a sanitorium
criminals, children mixed in, in the place called son of sorrows
his eldest, utterly sad, suicidal, beaten by unclean words, black fists
the rent money shoved down her small throat by he, he the reflection of he
she finally leaving
like the abandoned mother, drug after damned drug, not doing anything
let's try another 1, 2, 3, 4   shall we?   to see if they help you
fuck psychiatrists   fuck white psychiatrists   fuck canada
the youngest
in some alienated institution
where the city's insane
hang out to sleep, play cards
and piss in their beds
nightly
plan the misery of their lives
plan their runaway to the next neighbourhood, city, country, exotic world
oh sweet dreams, let their pills fill my blue veins
oh sweet dreams, let their pills fill my blaady brains
till i die
till we (all) die
he who had drunk himself
to sleep to forget the pain
the sink stained with pee, the blue nile flows as freely, but is more beautiful
he who had drunk himself
to sleep to forget the pain
of missing his homeland
south of the sahara
of missing his sister high in the mountains in the cape
of missing drinking with the men
at hotel kemo
of missing the big bottomless hole
painting the pulsator
that time at his god-daughter's twenty-first
the lucky key presented to her
the snap of him, mummy, the happy smiles then
even regretting what he had
done to his wife–his brutal tempers
for that had never left him
entirely
or his children

and he knew that
because the youngest   his only son
his first son
last son
son who received his blessed name
son who left
son who would leave
had secretly scolded, despised him
until all that mattered now
for the youngest
was to get the hell out
get the hell out
of house and home
and return back to africa
back to azania
back to zulu dances
back to biltong, curried dishes and a black
government that seemed to speak the people's language
but was just as corrupt as the previous
white one
had things changed in the country
for his people?
for the coloureds?
remember athlone, 1976
for the blacks?
for the malunde who still begged in hillbrow
and forgot their troubles in white plastic bottles
one whiff, one smile
one settler, one bullet
one whiff, one smile
one settler, one bullet
who was exile/d now?
how would the exile/d son
feel now
thirty years older/later
not really knowing
all of the brutalities
the urgencies
the callings
of country and mother
how would the exile/d son
feel now
after writers had left   jumped out of tall lonely buildings
because no one was permitted to read their words in the past
not one freshly printed angry page

not one permitted
into the country at war
and black revolutionaries   the communist manifesto carried like passports
had now returned, too, tearing down their signs that destroyed, that screamed
SLEG BLANKES!
would he take up their cause?
or was the cause forever abandonned?
would he cry (for freedom)
as loud as everyone else
as loud as madiba
as loud as madiba
would he?   could he?
or would he find himself
too westernized
too fucked up
everything that happened in his life
already had happened
and his time was but late
and his time had already come
ten, twenty, thirty years ago
alone   the son stood on the same
mountain top that overlooked
where prisoner 0221141011
prisoner of the nation
unwell nation which imprisoned him
on robben island, time for revolutionaries to break stones as presidents
on siqithini–the barren island where lunatics and lepers once roamed,
it jutting out into the deep green sea
the sea, its still beauty called out to unchain him
his cold stone cell no bigger than a small holding room
his toilet a grim reminder that life could get dreary
so dreary that death seemed inviting
that death seemed like the only way left out
the food tasting like urine, the beatings in straight-jackets beautifully sad
shock treatments in portugal, the asylums in england, germany
sept. 10, 1966 at 2:10 p.m. was his moment in history
verwoerd's blood, the blood of the nation, forcing itself to weep, maim, kill again
but he closed his eyes   he closed his eyes
and listened
to his heart pounding
to the sound of the sea, the waves breathing constantly
rhyming out his name silently, lyrically
as he walked down tyne street and smelled the sweet strong curry smells
smiled as dirty youngsters in torn clothes laughed about in open shacks
played in an old windowless automobile or slid down a walkway on milkcrates

and he saw the down-and-outs with their thin yelping dogs sleep in the open
smiled, talked to a woman with acorn-brown skin, greyed roots, wrinkled watery eyes
and later he decided to watch a film in the star bioscope with people
who looked like him, laughed like him, heard fights in the open chilly air
a young drunk woman tried to pick him up on hanover street, sharing biltong with him
he walked to the sea which brought his people here where they fished, washed, sang,
struggled
and then he walked to the embassador and danced with the moffies
in their fine flowing dresses and bouffants, twirling, twirling, twirling
yet he heard the roaring sound and felt the torturous heartache of the bulldozers at 6 a.m.
his people, crumbling, quickly gathering odds and ends to watch silently, mournfully
houses bulldozed one by one by one by one
hearts froze one by one by one by one
brown eyes closed then opened shedding tears
that would remember this hour, day, unending *pain*
and in that specific moment
of aloneness
he heard his mother's lovely, fragrant but desperate voice
sing out at sea point, the damp dampness all about
come home boetie
come home boetie
come home
and proudly now wearing her white, green, red and black beadwork on his head
she sang this   in between white domination, affirmative action, black domination
and this he remembered his father had sung
even after all of *those* books–piled high, not the ones on the crisis he was always given by
him
were found in his dark dim room, the room that screamed grief silently
even after all of *those* books–piled high, not the ones on the crisis he was always given by
him
were found in his dark dim room, the room that screamed grief silently
and he remembered a soup can had been thrown angrily, victoriously
narrowly missing daddy
years later the son came back
the son who shed his angry skin
the last son who remained on earth and asked forgiveness
the son who came to know his mother's voice
and it was daddy who soothed him   unusual as it was   unusual as it was
but the youngest stood in that church, chose and sang the songs that were to be sung at his
funeral
the songs that his people knew
the father's ashes were to be taken by the eldest
who couldn't manage to carry the heavy black urn
who couldn't manage to carry her heavy-hearted self
back to the homeland   back to her people   finally

back to kimberley to be buried beside
ouma and oupa
where important words were said at the old flat cemetary, it so hot that people cried
where coloured families gathered each sunday to lay down flowers, fresh tears
and hundreds of old folks who still read the *diamond field advertiser* all of those years
who knew the man, heard stories of him, remembered and laughed with him
ouma and oupa
whom the son
always wanted to know
because he had never known his wordless father
the father never quite knowing his father, either
exile/d   the man himself
like the son, longing   always
like the lonely, separated and meek mother
like the sisters separated, deserted by deathly darkness
and finally he decided
he would stay on
in africa, in the place he *belonged*, the land he knew, loved
stay on as long as he could
until his bills were too high, too high
until he was tired of too much rooibos tea and curried dishes at his relatives
he always he imagined he would
stay as long   find himself   his place
stay as long to meet the same kind of man, woman
recover his lost language, words–now set free
to scribble, speak, sing and remember his rhymes
words of freedom, hope, pain
the way he had always imagined
he would   it was in him
he knew it
the woman who wrote with thunder behind her ears
who was here, here and here   whispered it to him in a dream
now only to find it/him
now only to live each day as it should have been
as it should have been
for daddy
as it should have been
for mummy
as it should have been for
his sisters of the yellow masks
sisters still searching, still healing, still seedlings

words know pain & pleasure/
unmasking bodies, desires, oppression

Gauteng, South Africa, 1996

The drive to Riverlea seemed familiar. More familiar still to find the same old cars rusting in my uncle's front bare yard. The old faded Jaguar in which he had driven Kathy to Kimberley for the internment of my father's ashes stood there motionless. An old beige Benz looked equally deserted. Neither had the neighbourhood changed much, except for the fact that a squatter camp existed outside its outer edge, reminding all that many in the country still lived in abject poverty. These people were apartheid's victims, living in its shadow. The ANC seemed unwilling to remove them with their tin and cardboard homes. Too often the white government had driven them out, overseen by the fist of the police and army, forcing them to live in desolate areas. Smoke would emanate from each camp for miles around as garbage was burned in the wintertime to keep these African families warm.

I had many memories from ten years ago. The Africans huddled in woollen blankets as they worked at gas stations; the "twilight children" begging at robots or traffic lights as motorists stopped momentarily; the African mask that still hung in my kitchen my uncle must have found on one of his runs as he hauled garbage for the city (the African mask-carver must have called upon his ancestors to find just the "right" piece of wood and ward off evil spirits); praying with my godfather and his wife, and of course visiting Mummy, finally, finally.

Inside, the house looked unchanged. The walls had been painted a bland white, and clay hands in prayer were mounted on the back wall for all to see. The old bulky furniture, made of stinkwood with ball-and-claw feet, was just how I remembered it. Uncle Jacob was on the couch which faced the television. "She ached for you people, man, and now she's gone," he said. He was coughing badly, trying to speak at the same time. An old lung machine sat beside him. "The cyanide...in the mines where I worked there decades ago. My cough's from that," he mentioned to me, holding his chest fast and wiping the water from his tired eyes. Soon after I got hugs from all three kids who were now fully grown.

I was given a sweet naartjie to eat. Then I sat with my uncle after putting away my things down in one of the small bedrooms. The television blared: it showed a stocky, short, black-haired rugby carrier, clutching the ball tightly with his taped fingers as he tried to escape a brisk tackle. He was grabbed from all sides but his strides were too powerful, as he used his left arm and shoulder to fend off the last defender. My eyes were glued onto his solid upper legs–they were like thick muscular tree trunks, veined, lightly haired–with the blood rushing through them and on his tight black shorts that were hiked up to his crotch as he ran like a horse. How exciting!

"Norman, can you see if the Springboks are winning, man?" Uncle Jacob asked me excitedly, still coughing. I heard him pass gas, but pretended as if nothing had happened.
"Oh, I hadn't even noticed," I mumbled, turning my eyes away from the small television set.

Later, my auntie came to ask me about my sisters, as well as to talk about the funeral arrangements for the next day. Mark showed me the funeral program he had made using his computer at home. "We took this from a nice snap of your mom," he said proudly. It showed her smiling, with an old string of pearls draped around her neck. I thanked him and kept a few copies to show my sisters. My male cousins, I read, and I were to be some of the pallbearers from the hearse to the grave. My auntie and other women in the family would carry the coffin from the hearse to the church. This must have been a coloured tradition of some sort.

We travelled to an oefening or prayer meeting at John's house early that evening. It was good to see him because he had been such a good host some ten years earlier. He had put on some weight in the belly and looked older. Mary, his wife, came to meet me and Jeanette, their only daughter, now quite beautiful, smiled shyly at me. "Our sympathy Norman," Mary said, holding back tears and coming over to hug me. "It's good to be home," I said, and noticed that their bare living room had been quickly converted into a house of prayer, with a few friends sitting down on uncomfortable chairs that must have come from a number of their neighbours' homes. My close cousin Julia was sitting nearby. I gave her a wink and she smiled back. Several minutes later a youthful coloured lay preacher or oefeninghouder began the service.

I couldn't make out what he was saying (the Afrikaans was so utterly beautifully lyrical and hypnotic), but for some reason I thought that he was inexperienced and his small congregtion seemed as though it had become impatient with him to finish a sermon that was well over an hour, repeating several phrases too many times. It was the singing that I understood and rejoiced in. Even the young baby boy, who sat in his mother's arms next to me, smiled rejoicefully as the religious hymns known by many, word for word, were sung ryhthmically. For once I came to see who I was, not just spiritually, but culturally. My own culture, lost to being taken to another land, seemed far richer than being gay. Families were closer here. I could tell by how they interacted, knew each other and spoke the same language. Apartheid had also ensured familial bonding, for who else could one turn to in case of trouble?

I did not feel compelled to tell my auntie who I was, because I couldn't muster up any more emotional energy: my mother's death was upon me and that was all that mattered now. With the exception of my mental breakdowns that had forced me to quit university years ago, and Daddy's funeral three years prior, I hadn't been faced with having to question my own life, and what its future held for me. Would I suffer her same tragedy? Would I find love, maybe a feeling of spiritual happiness? Or would I continue my going to the baths and clubs–spiritual wildernesses unto themselves–only to remember the tragedy of not knowing her love? I had been living with loss for most of my life, and there was little I could do to face up to it. Coming to her funeral, I hoped, would end my own misery, finally–and pay homage to her lonely life.

The sun woke me the next day. I poured myself a cup of coffee, ate a koeksister and noticed that my relatives were already up, preparing for my mother's funeral. On the curb of the roadway near the old small house, I reflected on my thoughts, writing them freely in my journal, the warm rays on my body. Less than twenty-four hours earlier, I had been in Toronto watching the snow fly and people bundled up in coats, walking quickly on the cold concrete to catch the subway home. My spirit finally came to me to write the eulogy, and I asked my young cousin if I could use his old computer in his bedroom on which to write it. He soon left to pick up things for the wake. As I typed what would become a eulogy and tribute to my mother's long, tragic life without us, my fingers trembled across the keyboard, and the tears that were delayed finally came. I had to close the bedroom's door shut. But my writing continued, with me shaking as my tears fell gently, even over my fingers. Yet I felt excited to be in the country of my birth. People all seemed freer, and maybe I could feel this too despite my mother's passing.

The clash of dishes came from the kitchen near by and I could hear my auntie ask her daughter if she had ironed her clothes for the funeral. My tears made me feel better, lighter. *Mummy, don't worry, don't worry, I'm here now to be with and comfort you. I'm here now*–I whispered as I edited my words over and over again, thinking about her and the loss not only I had suffered, but also my sisters, my mother's sister, many cousins, neices and nephews. Towards the end of her life, life was made cruel by her loss of vision and few visitors, as my uncle also ailed.

The Poonees' funeral limousine arrived late, just after 2 p.m., and even then we had to wait a few blocks from the church until another funeral party proceeded out. I felt overly hot in my dark grey woollen suit, the very same one that I had worn to Daddy's funeral. The neighbourhood was different here–bleak, poorer and coloured families lived in three-story flats dotting the sad, even plains. People came out to stare at the funeral procession from the roadway, to see who we were and what the funeral was about. Children stopped playing and mothers with newborns stood nearby in front of single homes, looking on. Maybe it took them away from their own troubles. How strange death seemed: it excited one's imagination with awe and wonder. Coloured strangers came first singly, then by a few more to pay tribute to a woman they had not known. It wasn't the mourning procession of a nation, or for a princess who had died tragically, but of ordinary people for one of their own. Little did they know of her desperate existence.

I kept thinking of the photograph of me as a new baby on the settee in our house in Kimberley: bright-eyed, smiling, alert, probably looking at her as she nursed me. My life was destined to *be*, but I had no idea it would be *without* her. I hadn't cared when I came to see her ten years ago that she was ailing, that she lived in a madhouse. And still, now. I wanted to touch her, to call out her name, to comfort her.

Maybe at the time when we were saying good-bye to my mother at the Johannesburg airport as small children it was impossible for her to realize the supreme sacrifice that she was making: to see her children go without her–for good, and for her not to escape to a free country. But she remained. She stayed alive, hoping that we would never forget her, that we would again return her love. Come back to her. Nurture her. *Be with her.*

My mother was like other mothers who had been dealt terrible blows by apartheid. Steven Biko's wife, like Winnie Mandela, had been banned and sent to a desolate area in South Africa. Bessie Head left for Botswanna much earlier, never to return but to write of exile. My mother was as captivating and elegant as Ruth First, the white journalist who had been jailed for 117 days, then released and banned from practising journalism. First then enrolled in a librarian's course at Wits University. South Africa's librarians had to contend with banned book rooms in their libraries. Only two people at a time could see her in her home because of another ban. She finally left for Mozambique, during the Republic's dark days, with Joe Slovo, the head of the South African Communist Party and eventual Minister of Housing under Nelson Mandela's government. Opening what looked like a UN envelope that had been addressed to her, First was blown to pieces. Dulcie September also suffered the same fate years later in Paris as the chief ANC representative. Their deaths came quickly and foreshadowed the extent to which the apartheid state was willing to ensure that neighbouring countries, even recently independent Mozambique, would not harbour ANC guerillas. Both women died tragically, while my mother lived tragically. Women and children meant nothing to apartheid's police and secret agents. Blood spilled. Sjamboks split soft skin. Mothers cried for their jailed and tortured twelve-year-old children who would grow up to become tomorrow's revolutionaries. Their prayers to a merciful God went unanswered.

We finally made our way solemnly to the church, behind my mother's coffin, carried by women who nurtured and were nurtured by her. Parishoners greeted us, and laid eyes on the coffin now resting as we came into the hall. The attendants in dark suits unscrewed the wooden top of the coffin, exposing my mother's face for us to see. The casket stood alone on the dark blue rug, its three silver handles planted on either side. A number of people passed without staying too long at her side, but when I came up to her, I sensed that I might not know her. Her name was emblazoned on a silver name plate on the casket's top, as if to say her life held importance. The attendants came to me to ask if everything was alright, and I came to. After several seconds I observed that her gentle, withdrawn face, now pale pink, surrounded by beautiful mauve, white and pink flowers. She looked as though she had lost all of her weight and innocent beauty. But then again, she was a petite woman. My mother's eyes were closed but I finally saw her in me; the gentle flow of brown eyelashes and eyebrows, a mouth now closed tight, as if she were in a deep, deep, quiet sleep. I pressed my lips to the window of the casket and kissed her good-bye. *Peace at last. No more pain.* I stood with her, laying my eyes on her for one final moment, then snapped a portrait of her that I could bring home to my sisters. I wondered briefly if my parents had ever longed for each other.

During the isibongo or praise poem, I could remember speaking of my mother's love of family, even of her simply adoring delicious cream cakes, and of her longing for us, and us for her when I spoke during the English service. The final quote came from Kahlil Gibran: "If you would indeed behold the spirit of death, open your heart wide unto the body of life. For life and death are one, even as the river and the sea are one." A smartly dressed man approached me quietly outside as we talked to guests. "My name is Makhaya, and I knew your mother at the sanitorium," he said to me softly, as he extended his ebony hand. He had this incredibly sad, reflective look on his face, eyes warm with feeling.

"I had written to Blanche every now and then. Your mother may have mentioned you to me, as I was also at the East Rand briefly, but then recovered. We kept posting each other over the years. Actually, more was sent by me. But it became more difficult as she became ill over the last while. My job as editor at a large Jo'burg newspaper has kept me occupied recently," he told me quietly. "I told your mother as she lay there in the coffin, 'Laga ngo Xolo, Uli sebenzele ntombi ya se Afrika: Izwe la ko Kweno.' It means 'Rest in peace. You have served your country, daughter of Africa.'" Eyes stared at us. These were words only a true friend could say, I thought, and I thanked him. "Maybe I can see you in the week," I said–but there would be such a commotion with me going to see this relative and that one, I didn't know if there would be time. As my auntie asked me to accompany the family to the hearse so we could go to the graveyard, I waved so long, wondering later who this dear man was. What he had meant to my mother...

There was a sense of relief after we had carrried her heavy coffin from the black hearse to the gravesite where it was hoisted up on a shiny silver bed, prior to it being lowered into the deep grave. A group of us sang hymns. The minister spoke solemnly from his Bible: "Everlasting God, help us to realize more and more that time and space are not the measure of all things. Love does not die, and truth is stronger than the grave. God of our strength, in our weakness help us; in our sorrow comfort us; in our confusion guide us. Without you our lives are nothing; with you there is fullness of life for everymore." Light rain soon fell.

The flat cemetery was enclosed by a high stone fence. Fresh graves were all about us. Mine heaps and lone angular trees dotted the surrounding area, while overhead there was a cobalt-blue sky. Some thirty years previously, my aunt and mother had stood here sorrowfully, burying their German father, my oupa, a shopkeeper. A cousin from another family dressed in black cotton pants and blouse, with the wind sweeping her hair, read from the program and sang. She stood there, holding a young coloured girl close to her–alone. Maybe this was the first time the child understood what death meant. We were all very downcast, quiet. And in that moment of aloneness, we came together as a family and a people.

The casket was finally lowered by African attendants in their indigo blue overalls, settling in its final resting place in the red earth, and after we had all strewn rose petals over it, the men in the family took up shovels and began to scoop the earth that had been dug up into the the awaiting grave. When Shaka's attendant and favourite imbongi and praise singer MxHamama ka-Ntendeka returned to see his master dead, he broke out and flung himself onto Shaka's grave, asking to be allowed to follow the king to his death. His death was brutally agreed to. Had I not seen Mummy ten years ago, I also would have wanted to fling myself in her yet-unmarked grave.

The digging offered something that I had not expected. What seemed like such a simple task became a way for us to let go of our emotions physically, a collective catharsis in digging and scooping, digging and scooping, with the light rain still comforting us. We took off our jackets and rolled up our sleeves, taking turns in freeing gravel with our shovels from the hill of earth, and moving it closer to the gravesite so that others could help bury my mother's coffin. When we had finished our digging some forty minutes later, flowers from the church were placed on top of the mound of earth. A tombstone would come later as the earth still needed to settle.

a moffie night out

Dancing alone, I had met a beautiful chestnut black man with braids on the dance floor of the so-called leather bar in Jo'burg. Tired and anxious about being in unfamiliar territory, I felt that it was nearly time to go. A few more men arrived, followed by two coloured drag queens, who glanced at me as I stood at the top of the stairs, close to the dance floor, decorated by cheap Christmas things hanging from the ceiling. They came back and went down a flight of stairs, disappearing into a doorway. Maybe it led outside. I wanted some fresh air and picked up my posters, one of *Two Straight Queers*, a gay play staged at the Market Theatre, and the other, the *I Turned to Safer Sex* Poster from OUTREACH on Esselen Street in Hillbrow. The latter and usual thing was depicted, a cute naked black man in jack boots. I had taken both from the washroom wall of the other bar, Champions, which I had just visited. No one noticed, luckily.

My new surroundings were indeed outside, save for the many bars that were on the veranda, as I made out the street and light traffic from below. The two moffie queens introduced themselves to me very mannerly. Rachel sported a lengthy, tight, emerald-green velvet dress and a red boa while her friend Leoness had that 70s bitchy look, complete with hoop earrings, more than enough make-up and three-inch heels.

"You want some dagga?" one of them asked me after she lit it and took a slow puff.

"Okay," I said, taking hold of the joint, nicely referred to them as Gina. It tasted strong but did absolutely nothing for me.

"So you're from Canada, then," her courteous friend asked me.

I nodded yes.

"It's not easy being a drag queen," Leoness confided as she fixed her hair and dress, cupping her fake boobs to centre them properly. "We make our living singing at birthday parties and at Trends, another bar." Both of them said that they had lived in Hillbrow for a few years.

Remembering that I was whisked here by private taxi and told not to get out until I was in front of the club, I asked one: "You're not afraid of the crime, then?"

"It's as good as any other place. Although some of the Cloras whom I call friends don't want to come out alone at night."

"Well, I'm glad to have found my way to the club," I added. "It was such a battle to get here, even my relatives wanted to escort me. I had to lie and say that I was meeting a friend of my cousin's here. I couldn't imagine my relatives walking into this place with me."

"On the weekend this place is packed, man. We jorl up a storm, with leathermen, pretty white things, exhibitionists, even the occasional lettie and shebeen queen," Rachel went on.

I looked around. Hillbrow was quiet save for the taxis and a few people milling on the street below. My cousin had taken me downtown earlier and the sidewalks were crowded with Africans selling everything from shoes to Celine Dion CDs. He laughed, "Oh South Africans love her, but can't understand her French songs." Jo'burg was now completely African. More "down market" according to coloureds and other non-whites. Whites had now left for the affluent suburbs such as Sandton, deeply segregated just like American cities.

I returned to the moffie queens, who looked out of place here.

"Do they come, too?" I asked inquisitively. "Africans, I mean."

"Natalies...the blacks–they come if they can afford it man."

"It must be hard for them," I added. "I thought they still didn't come out to the bars."

"It's getting better, I mean, even ou Shaka, King of the Zulus, was a blaady moffie!" claimed Rachel.

"Oh, fok now! I don't believe it," said her feline friend.

"Years ago, as a varsity student, I was doing some research for a history class, man. I think he was a mlandwana or illegitimate child of a promiscuous mother who had him when she failed to keep her thighs together in the hlobonga manner. Sure, he was a great warrior. Had a lisp, possibly a stutter. Hilda–you know. I read that he might be a 'latent homosexual.' And he avoided women and put to death men who made women in the isigodlo pregnant. He wanted no heirs who might rise up and kill him."

"Sounds fascinating," I said, not wishing to interrupt.

"There was word that he even killed his own mother, driving a small assegai into her side."

"That's reva–revolting," her friend commented, brushing her long hair aside.

"Shaka was very remorseful. And ordered that in honour of his mother's death, no crops should be planted and the entire Zulu nation was not to have sexual intercourse for one year. If that wasn't all, any woman bearing children and her husband would be put to death."

"It sounds as if he hated sex. Not a *real* moffie!" Leoness echoed.

"He liked to dress smartly," Rachel smiled. "Even wore a golden kilt and long blue feather from the tail of a lory bird in his headband."

"I don't know if the Zulus would want people to know this part of their history, if that's the case, that their fearless founder, king and ruler could have been a moffie," I told both of them, not wishing to spoil their reinterpretation of history. Then again ou Cecil Rhodes was known to have preferred young men.

The two looked like they had had too much to smoke. They began to fight over something.

"Jou ma se poes!" (your mother's cunt!), Leoness reeled, grabbing her friend's bag from her. It was nearly as bad as hearing an insult from a hijra like "Go suck your husband's sugarcane!"

"She wants more. A cilla," Rachel said, letting go of the small red handbag.

They soon departed, leaving me stranded and alone, thinking of my return to Canada after seeing my mother's casket descend deep into the African earth.

***

Julia, my close cousin, followed me outside of the hotel where we had all come to dance. So my secret was finally exposed. We said to my aunt's children and my other cousins that we were leaving for a club after we had all danced, talked and laughed about life in South Africa and Canada. And they didn't mind. My lips hid a smile at her low-cut, white blouse, exposing her round cleavage. *Was that for me?* A kiss and warm hug from me for her beautiful parting gift, a gold ring that fit perfectly. It was nearly as if we were married, that my secret was her's.

We arrived at Champions, now busier than the first night I was here. I still remembered how I had shared *Exit*, the gay paper I bought for a few rand. Many Africans couldn't afford it.

Julia and I finally made it to the dance floor after a drink and standing around talking. Then a man my age hovered close to us. Cute, I thought. He brushed beside me on the dance floor and smiled, showing off his muscles poking in his tight T-shirt.

"You from here, then?" he asked. "I've never seen you before."

"No–Canada," I answered. He said that he was from Soweto and that his name was Alfred.

Julia smiled at him, us.

"I'm amazed that the country has eleven national languages, now."

"That's true. You have your own Inkatha in Canada?"

"Canada has two languages, and we can barely get along. We've got the Bloc Québéçois!"

He came a bit closer so that he could hear me better. The music was loud. "The new South Africa is a place for African women to do much better and achieve. Have you seen Felicia Mabuza-Suttle's show yet?"

"I saw one show and the audience was very responsive. I just wish she'd just shut up a bit."

"It's a common complaint. But she's our Oprah, here." He soon sipped from his beer nearby. "Felicia's taking the nation's pulse. She knows what commuters in trains and elbow-lifters in shebeens want to hear," he remarked.

"I see."

"The Affirmative Action program–even the one on gays–were very popular. She doesn't wear traditional outfits. She's a real role model for the younger ones. A new spirit of hope and ubuntu exists here in South Africa. Everyone is here now. In Yeoville, you can eat Nigerian egusi soup, Congolese mabumu a pepe soup or Ethiopian wat, a kind of stew. And *Drum* even reported that a white gay male couple adopted a black baby!"

"Really!"

Alfred continued, "South Africans–my relatives–don't think much of homosexuality. They just want to see what is happening in our underpants to see if we have a penis and a vagina. If boys think another boy is gay, they will pull off his clothes to see what's down there. They think we are stabane or hermaphrodites, if we say we are gay."

The club's thick smoke made my eyes weary. It was only 12:30 and Julia asked if we could leave early. I told Alfred it was time to go, even though I wanted to speak more, be with him. I finally shook his hand. Squeezed him. My head ached and I drank from my half-finished beer. We bid Alfred good-bye again. The African bouncer found a cab, and it was plummeting rain outside. The motor-car slowly made its way to Riverlea. "Oupa, watch the traffic line, you are going over it, né!," Julia announced to him as she leaned from the back seat, trying to see where he was taking us. The old man still seemed as if he were sleeping a bit. He must have been working too long, too hard, the poor guy. The rain continued to pelt down to the extent that the old car was now slowly moving in between gushing rivers of water on the dark slippery road.

My mind was on my trip back home the next day and how I had missed my mother and culture all of these long, hard years. Now to lose it all over again. Mummy's funeral and *final* death–preparing for it psychologically and my travel back home had taken too much out of me.

distance running

men leave me
as quickly as they enter my small
home (in which i escape)
and each man i remember
each encounter, however brief
each arrival, night that was spent with them
was but a single poem, a single passionate four pages
a thoughtful deliberate untangling of
our short-lived love affair
for men do want you
but they do not need you
for men want some one
but no one at all
for all men betray and fear death–always
and in that final hour
when cum, shit and saliva
mix with unsure tears of joy
orgasms of death seem
just a moment away
they say to you
let's not exchange numbers
it will just spoil the moment...
as they walk out of your door
shoe laces left untied,
back still wet from a soothing hot shower
spent condoms and used towels lay about
cigarettes smoulder in an ashtray
smoke whispering slowly away
always dating
always searching
always *nowhere*
everyone wants the same *white* thing
but you do not know who *he* is, who he *really* is
and you realize that dating is for fools
fags know that too often
only to drink and fuck their troubles away
lonely foggy nights   nights that are endless
unknown, dark swirling rivers tell us that

Dear God, March 10, 1992

Issac and I were together intimately on Sunday for the LAST TIME. We had a beautiful day or what seemed beautiful–brunch, a visit to screen a film at his friend's house, then to the YMCA, and church for me and finally dinner at his place, where we talked, held hands and made love like it was the final time... I even got him to promise me that we'd go away somewhere together for a few days around Easter, but after calling him back Monday evening, he didn't seem inclined. He had retreated to his usual nonchalant self and seemed indifferent. Maybe there was still a chance we could see each other for a day. Easter was still a month away. I told him over the phone that I was feeling low, down-hearted. That we didn't have "combined interests." He agreed without a fight, which I expected, and suggested we not see each other for a long time. Maybe it's for the better. I miss him, God, like I've missed a strong brother. He can be kind, honest most of the time, but he also hides himself through words and deeds. Issac is also hard-working and more intelligent than most. The bugger even makes me laugh, and it's those little things I miss about him: the way he wears those ugly old black boots to keep his feet warm in the winter, or the way he has to carry his gym things in a hand-held bag. "My back gets too sore," he always says. Those sensuous dark eyes, his soft luxuriant scent; I shall also not forget easily. I can't live without him it seems at times. We can't live with ourselves, either. The spring rains should come soon, and maybe that will be the time of my healing.

The crunch of lettuce leaves, sliced English cucumber, Spanish onions and fresh tomatoes with olive oil, lemon juice and a pinch of lemon and pepper dressing for my salad, makes me think of him. He was the one who taught me how to prepare it while I held onto his side, bit his ear and listened to his campy stories in the kitchen. A tangy spicy bitterness sweeps over my tongue.

One bright September Sunday, 1999

"Just gimme a kiss, come on. Just one kiss," he pleaded as he looked around to see that no one was looking at us. This, as we were in the locker room of the YMCA, changing.

"No," I said, attempting to get past him to go to the pool.

"Just one–it doesn't have to be much, just one. Hey–what's wrong anyway?"

"No!"

"Most South Africans are so much warmer, you know..."

"Not this one," I bellowed. Smiling to myself, I left him. The black brothers in red shirts quietly roll in another trolley of fresh white towels. Silent hungry eyes from pinkish-white-skinned men pierce at me through the hot hissing steam of the sauna. Eyes closed, I pretend not to notice them while I do my stretches. Back drips. I wipe my brow. *Up*, over, *up*, over.

here/now

here
in that forlorn place where i came, scribbled something of you in a new book of poetry i
just bought, your second-hand blanket–holed and blackened by time–strewn, left behind
on the cold filthy ground inside only to find rest (cameras on you), to sleep, undisturbed,
worried–cigarette butts on the carpet, while my young afroed friend upstairs told me that
he was on e, f, g or special k ("if i get touched all over it's like getting fucked," he said
with that weird look on his face, lips turned up in a funny way, eyes in another
head/space), as i spend time looking for love only to wack off in the dark dingy jerk-off
room as white men on the screen do their shameless thing (the filthy darkrooms in club 58
in jo'burg not that far away) while you exchange food for sex just to make it from one
day to the next

*give your heart to the lord. repent! lord be merciful, from life unto death. the lord comes
to save sinners. he is the son of god. pray with me. praise you! heaven is yours child.
hallelujah!*

here
in that forlorn place where your friends on the cold steps ask old white men when they
come out of these heart-racing doors for change, knowing that it is a place they arrive for
passionless nights where nothing happens but moans, gasps, panting for breath in the deep
of dark with a perfect stranger, or for them to walk up and down long dark alleyways in
frayed white towels searching, waiting endlessly (nights can be like that especially when
full moons come out), then showering away diseases in plain view of others, only leaving
to come down four long flights by elevator in the government building (gentlemen do not
smile at each other after they have sex with strangers) and leave you a tip to redeem
themselves while you sleep and dream of black things which remind you of your past:
beatings, rapes, cigarette burns on your ass, scoldings

*give your heart to the lord. repent! lord be merciful, from life unto death. the lord comes
to save sinners. he is the son of god. pray with me. praise you! heaven is yours child.
hallelujah!*

here
in that forlorn place, old crinkled newspapers strewn about, words on grey walls indecipherable which not even you can make out nor your friends can read, i have seen you in
my dreams though you do not resemble the homeless mother and sisters i left behind

here
in that forlorn place, i have called out your name but cannot hear you or see your invisible
eyes as they look downcast on me, my cheap new clothes, new 70s look, sad brown south
african eyes and clipped hair that i couldn't afford

*blessed are the poor in spirit: for theirs is the kingdom of heaven, blessed are they which
do hunger and thirst after righteousness: for they shall be filled here in that forlorn place.*

56

dream 1,005: tuesday december 23

walking along a beautiful path, along a slow winding river in the deep woods
she, softly slurping a vanilla milk shake
her dark brow filled with sweet sweat
the sun upon us from all around, strong, luxuriant, warm
i do not know her by sight
the cool breeze blows freely and gently
her long ravishing dark hair waves towards my face
look at these, i say to her as we walk slowly, pointing to her delicate chest
thoughts of cherry brown nipples that will bloom in my mouth
she smiles, taking my hand, as any high-school sweetheart
we must first pass train tracks
that run endlessly and become flowers
and then we dodge underneath heavy lines
unknown voices surge like electricity
destination unsure
this ain't the underground railroad
echoes of strangers–other couples talking
secluded cabins come to view soon
i've been here but haven't
no money on me but an interac card
whiles she holds out a gold card
and we spend a night or two
and bathe in each others' warm waters
as children, we two play, snuggle
and discover our childish ways
touching her pebbled back
i find myself swimming through ice-blue shallow streams
with cherry blossoms scattered throughout
as my school-age sisters dive playfully off my strong back
softly treading the dirtied ground below the mirrored surface

waiting

he wanted men
like drinking beer and smoking (and that was hourly)
his fresh face, frightened
as he lit another smoke in the dark stale cloudiness of the club
inhale   gulp   exhale   inhale   gulp   exhale
with his cigarette pack tucked neatly in the back of his briefs by the elastic
his clothing check in his short white socks
angry pecs pumped over and over again
one hundred other faces   lit by one hundred other meaningless matches
men everywhere, eyes darting everywhere in the deep deep blackness
he looked around anxiously, in clean white underwear, swaying to the bumping beat
turning to see
and every week it was feverishly the same
meeting another new guy who had a lover   heart racing   pupils dilating
or an interesting couple from germany   oh that one   the baths on his birthday
he'd always return
especially upstairs
sitting on benches twenty years old
that had seen semen, beer and sweat
ingrained on them, by men coming here, fading faces
with jerk-off videos overhead of hard white men and no longer innocent hairless holes
sort of like another passing moment
in history
another boring spectator event
on a sunday in which a straight couple would play with their children
or watch a neil diamond concert at the gardens
yeah, one couple did come in, asking if they could have a drink here
but i guess when they saw men taking off their clothes in exchange for leather and
jock straps
they knew this wasn't like home and left
luckily they hadn't come up to see naked fifty-year-olds playing pool in running shoes
either
white dry skin folding over white dry skin
he wanted men like drinking and smoking (and that was hourly)
arching hips   driving, driving   on his king size bed with its blue-green covers
the same bed that only knew too many strangers   a teacher, a friend of a friend,
an ex-lover
at thirty, he knew he wanted men
like drinking beer and smoking (and that was hourly)
at thirty, he heard his tribal callings
the callings of hasty demonstrations, handing out the same familiar notices at
church street
the callings, demandings by the old white tribe
the callings of old familiar white ways that would suffocate   finally castrate him

26 B

up burnhamthorpe
we go, accordioned bus
into the burbs called
miss-iss-aug-a
where indians once roamed
how much longer
i ask, how much longer?
doing this, journeying so far
only brown faces
noire faces
old wrinkled faces
those with slanted eyes, queers
and sleepy students
on the accordion bus
bending, bending bus
they look out of the window
waiting to be assimilated
sudden stops
fucking nasty driver!

the concrete, concrete road
is the flat hard stagnant ocean
which encircles this entire city
the bus moves on, creepingly so
nothing but cars, alive, speeding
stopping, turning, watching
skateboarders on stretching sidewalks, big pants, b-boys

people still staring outside
endlessly
thinking of families, pains, losses
in sleepy suburbia
while i am getting over ghonorrea
and an itch   ouch!

take these said the asian doctor
and out i ran with a prescription
from the wellesley while it was still up
only to catch the third act
of an opera–too european for me
even though i knew something of roman history

fear the living, not the dead

cooked like his santa marian mother, making ten loaves of bread at once...she had nine to feed
takes a long, long drag...before puffing, pausing–my ex blew his head off, his lover was
blown to pieces, too...mother killed herself, mother killed herself, when he was seven...
hell, it's fucking ice-cold in here...fuck, where's the heat?
oh, *that*–the farm, it was always mother-fuckin minus ten or somethin, you'd never
survive there, just a wood stove, i miss the wild horses, and the snow was so pure you'd...
his hands were soft as feathers. when we watched that action movie he said that subtitles made him
sleepy. a soothing shower to get the smoke off him. that body i craved, wanted to see, hold
mind if...i join you, i asked, first feeling his smooth soapy ass in that old tub and shower
stall he put together in the kitchen...me already seeing my clothes scattered on the floor
sure, come on in...(giggles as if he were the same guy i met in montreal, still cute, hot as ever...)
my shaved cock was already *up*, as it took less than a breath to get my winter socks, army
pants, light grey sweater i bought in kensington off, hop in, hop in...the darkness inviting
rubbed him hard, rubbed him hard, licked his watery, hot firm back, hairless like a young girl
honey, i don't get hard standing up, i hear...i'm dead from the waist down...the soap falls,
he bends over. bites on those buttocks, more bites–on both cheeks, a smack. ouch!
yeah, i've got some black in me, he says. shows me the pictures: portugal had the largest slave
trade in the world; even a slave house, under my relative's mansion...nineteenth-century, i hear.
kisses on the blue black bed, kisses on the blue black bed, more bites...he turns away...
sshh.sshh/shadow turns shh.shh/soft shusshes   sings sadly like amalia rodrigues
we stop temporarily, he's bored i can tell...*show me how you fuck...show me*...heaves his
hips. you've got energy, energy that explodes, i said, and it's kind of fucking scary!!
a lover said the same thing...throws boyish smiles at me, another slow cigarette...end of the
month at work, he adds, lights another...smoke snakes and fizzles as if we just came, but didn't...
i've got to run to the bathroom, i end. seconds later pills go down, a small drowsy orange
one drops by mistake into the cold dark drain–fuck, he doesn't know about them–yet.
we roll like children in bed from 1, 2, 3, 4...deep sleep...cold dreams...warm as lambs, entwined
10 a.m., covers off...a bite of his flat hairless nipple...a grab of his thick horse's hairy leg.
honey–that nine-inch thing ain't gonna go in me!   blankets off. brrrrrh–it's fucking freezing...
shh.shh.shh., switches sides, laughs, my hips up, my hand on my pulsating thing moving,
viagra stare, a slight slant on his thin silvery shaft, the green glowing bed-light leads the way. i
don't do deep kissing, i say. here–let me teach you how to kiss...a portuguese woman taught me...
him: i can only do 69s if i'm fuckin drunk...that's how i met my other ex, fell for him in a
week...oh fuck, guess i had a wife, he cooked, cleaned, watched jerry springer...we got fat...
up for breakfast...pillsbury croissants and omelette never tasted so good...we're a couple
already; hell, i put my arms around his waist like i used to do with the jewish filmmaker...
listen, we've made no commitments...the other guy's coming soon, he interrupts, rushing, puffing
nearly 12 already,...i'll leave, i say...i don't mind you dating–kinda weird i thought.
no–stay, no–stay...another cup of coffee; he's cute, says he...the geneticist who's to pick him up.
i loved someone–hiv, another ex, maybe that scared people off...found a bag of white stuff...
oh, that's why you'd get tested so much. my spooked eyes look out the door. *gotta leave*

going and finding a home

i have walked
the same lonely streets
you did
only one thousand times more
one thousand times harder
porn shops on christopher street in the village, the wall-street sauna at 2 a.m.
b-boys skateboarding in lincoln mall, smiling hermân–the tanned dancer in calvins
says "enter" at his door with sizzling pizza in hand
f-market street cars on market street, danny the "foreign student" sporting a
japanese tattoo
he's on his pager again; who is that gentleman he's calling?
enough time for him to show me the sunny-cool san francisco bay, alcatraz,
the golden gate
with us frolicking, kissing, licking, frolicking then dinner for two in the castro
the mile-hike up halstead, that bathouse and its large leather room i peak in, leaving
a boring hour later
i have walked the same lonely streets
you did only
one thousand times more
one thousand times harder
in the same city
alone/with men from bars and baths
at 2 a.m.
in the hushed morning
for company or sex
golden leaves die ceremoniously
on unsure icy sidewalks, streets,
i have now realized
that game of death and life
can no longer
continue
and that my flame
is low   so low
that i sing
the same lullabies
sauntering home
that my father
hummed to me
in the early morning hours
and nights
of my spoiled
childhood
mummy where are you?   i want out.

and yet another prescription from my shrink

I.

CHLROPROMAZINE (Thorazine)
Preparations: Tab 10, 25, 50, 100, 200 mg
Adult Dosage
1. Excessive anxiety, tension and agitation: 10-25 mg PO tid (in severe cases may increase dosage by 20-50 mg semi-weekly until patient becomes calm and cooperative) **Indications**: Management of psychotic disorders, control of nauseau and vomiting, relief of intractable hiccups
2. FUCK PSYCHIATRY

II.

i saw coloured pictures of the capsules in dosages in a new medical textbook that some shrink probably read for bedtime reading. the bright orange, round flat pills that i placed in jiffy bags along with other ones–smaller, bigger, different hues. these would be pulled out as i searched for them in bars or baths, their dirty washrooms–unpolished watery floors making you want to jump-step them, and then one hour before leaving, i'd find clean water to belt down my drugs that would foolishly be mistaken by some young queer for ecstasy. 60 minutes, 3660 seconds later, and many heartbeats grinding to bumping music with my hands in the air, stretching, reaching up, up, shirtless, ass wiggling, feet twirling, dancing, running my pain away as girlish david hops in the dark in fur boots to and fro like a free negro (but this place is so white i yawn). drowsy, getting drowsy, drowsy, getting drowsy. no, i was not taking the green-white one called prozac, the stuff of self-help titles of books, the drug of choice of psychiatrists (the pharmaceutical companies have held their hands for too long now). there was carbamezapine, the small white thing that went down my throat. *have i been forced to swallow my troubles away?* hell, where was the second little one? it must have hit the ground bouncing somewhere in a dark corner. shit, it's dirty. i'll have to wipe it on my socks. memories of leaving university in deep black days when daddy said, "boetie, please don't leave varsity," trying to cuddle me but not wanting to talk about my fate, her fate, our cruel fate and his–again. the long lonely cold walks to the albion library in mournful snow storms, my safe place to pencil pictures of african elephants. memories of my father speaking softly, warmly, kindly to me. a soothing gentleness i had soon forgotten.

III.

ect, etcetera is the head-hammering stammer of their instruments against us. they don't see the fear that fastening our heads to the two small round plates called electrodes have–electriCITY passing through them, us like this fuckin city don't want us. FUCK WAR, FUCK MARRIAGE, FUCK YOU–i told the shrink when it was all over, when he sat their fuckin listening again like i wasn't there. the last bit of our fuckin therapeutic bullshit hour was over with. i was just a hole to my husband, like i was money in the bank to the shitty shrink, his green eyes piercing at me.

at 27

one boring afternoon
she, the youngest
with long rivers of braids
while
studying
at the library
piled books, unspoken words, ideas–sighs
breathing in the
stale air of european history,
came accidentally
across an ancient text
of african women's
poetry, mentioning the afar
that contained
a hand-written
letter,
beautifully
penned,
looking to be
from someone
named
althea
to another
named
grace
whispered words
elegantly spoken
simply said:
me   you
love   us
i   felt
your   body
the soft colour
of coal
beautiful
still   as i
lay   awake
thinking
of   you
yours in love,
always   A.

this foggy
day
now clear
for she had
always
secretly
quietly
momentarily
thought of her
sex   sisters
woman-identified woman
blackafricanwoman
loving
blackafricanwoman
this way
for she had
always desired
to meet not
a boy   friend
but a womanfriend
in class
so that they could
secretly cuddle
study, feet touching
they two study
maru
and play with their
zulu love beads
bright
red, blue, white
letters of sorrow
happiness
and love
becoming
familiar
with un/discovered territory
their ebony bodies
embracing
sweet caresses
let us flow as one oshun!
let us lie as one oshun!
and so she
took this fragrant letter

and kept it in
her shirt pocket, sealed secretly
her petite ochre cherry nipples
raised like young spring buds
from the cold
chilly air
of the vent
where she
was sitting
a woman librarian
studying her all this time
dressed so
conservatively
as to suggest
little sexual flirtation
while the young
student
went home
to touch herself
after
taking
a hot bubbly bath
moaning, sighing
moaning, sighing
dreaming of the
mysterious note
wet with persperation
as her small ripe breasts
rose and fell
in wind-swept waves
the gentle
fragrant foam
between
her forceful
brown thighs
leaving the sheets
soaked,
endless oceans
endless fields of oceans
endless moments
of ecstasy
...oh...
how she sighed

of goddesses and gods

She would be the only woman he would marry, sleep with, talk to in the hush of the gentle night, suckle her breast, her fertile milk feeding him with pleasant exuberant thoughts that remained with him all of his life. Her protection of her loved one from Him could only last as long as he was of a particular age, and finally she let go of him, waving good-bye (he could not see her decades of tears, but felt them always). But he did return after such a long arduous journey, and each and every dawn she would silently enter his room, watch him sleep as he lay there, legs splayed half apart, manhood showing slightly, dark crinkled hair surrounding the thing which brought her only sorrow. One bright morning, he eyed her hushed presence, coffee cup in hand, and she pretended to be looking at his clothes–the untidy suitcase, straightening things up, old musty toys here and there below on the floor.

"I'll be out as soon as I change, and then we can have a big breakfast. It will be lekker, né," he yawned, pulling up the small bit of white sheet over himself without much care. Sunlight beamed through the burglar barred windows holding faded drapes that had not been changed for some time in the small home. She scooted out, leaving him finally. He had thoughts of her, of missing life with her. For some strange reason, he wondered what it would be like to have met someone as ravishing as she, for he had seen the snap of her at age twenty-one, his age now, as she held the first. He imagined unclothing her. Touching her warm, brown wrinkled body, taking the timelessly radiant breasts that had fed him for but a few years into his soft palms, lips, caress her for eternity. Discover her and her people, hoping that she would invite him with open adoring arms. And the flow of disrupted memory made his firm hand move faster, slower, faster, slower–legs tensing against the rickety bunk bed.

Heart racing, and then slowing, he lay there quietly thinking of seeing Them naai in their bed as his eyes caught them in the still darkness centuries ago, and then He got up suddenly to ride to the mines. And of the time he came to His bed (he had forgotten how close they were at first), cuddled up to him, later waking up to quietly rub himself hard, even harder against His hairy leg. It was the first time he felt a flow out of him that arose like an unknown frightening river. Fear turned to joy, smiling. Silence from the old man, snoring so. He fell asleep, holding onto Him.

Coming out of the hot bath, changing into his summer shorts, he heard her call out, "Kiss me!", as she listened and sung to the radio, swaying back and forth. Back and forth. And so he did kiss her, he did gently, hiding his squishy plaything. An innocent remorseful smile. The land appeared different here, with mine dumps in the distant blue skies, towering above everything else. He had suddenly come to realize that this was what he wanted–to see her, embrace her forever, yet blaming Him for Her deathly misery, still.

the kiss

holding your sweet chocolate thighs
slightly wide
me still kneeling
as you stand above me
breasts dangling, wanting caresses and bites
my lips meet yours
petalled
covered
closed
then opened
a gentle nibble
makes you *jump* and arch your
sculpted back
a brief giggle
soft oozing sighs
then you
kiss me
in the same way
your cassolette
still covers me
all over
and after
i whisper to you
sweetly
est-que vous le désirez
...from behind?
with rapturous moments
of dominique
still on my mind
dominique who passed
out
a silent explosion
a soft still death
right after our
frenzied lovemaking

she took me to see a performance

sitting close together, legs nearly touching
i show her my whole life, pensive
palms facing inward
i pull
my petite delicate hands
moving them briskly,   briskly
together   and   apart
together   and   apart
she seems to understand
by nodding quietly
the lonely dancer takes to the darkened stage

68

what the water gave us

I counted out sometimes as I swam at the Y. Stretch, stroke, kick, stroke. Breathe. Stretch, stroke, kick, stroke. Breathe. Passing funny little kids who were flutter-kicking in the lane beside me, I made the final kick and stretched to the end, turned around again and got on my back. Tilting my head far back into the water allowed my entire body to lie parallel to the wavy surface. I counted my strokes out again. Water gushed onto my goggles, and I breathed out hard, letting air in and out as I could feel my abs working. In between looking up at the coffered and partially windowed ceiling towering high above, through which sunlight beamed down into the pool's wavy surface thus hitting me in my left goggled eye as I backstroked straight ahead, I began to see and imagine her. *The cold hard metal stud and soft point of her nipple collided into one as my tongue circled these. We were swimming in each others waters: me licking her thighs, she the inside of mine, darting her tongue in and out of my navel, descending swiftly just above my shaved pubic hair. I was as hard as a young boy and licked the inside swirl of her ear, coming down to bite her full lips and slide my body ever so gently onto hers. She grew excited, heated–sighing out. Smooth legs, her sensual limbs, wrapped around me delicately.*

Nearly bumping my head, I reached the other side of the pool and came back to reality again. I had had these thoughts about Mina for some time now. We met casually at a friend's dinner party. I fell for her thick black hair and soft gentle eyes. As a medical librarian she seemed to know a lot about AIDS research, leaving the West Coast and her stern Japanese mother for Toronto. Sure I knew she liked women, but I found out later that there were men in her past. But she didn't say much about them. I started inviting her to my place for dinner–oh yes, those sumptuous balcony meals in the summer, with my flowers blooming, the sun hitting us into the face so much so that we needed sunglasses to see each other. We double-dated a few times, did brunch at Slack Alice's on Church, and danced until the wee morning hours at Tango. I even liked to shop for her, finding a vintage knitted charcoal halter (size 6) at Asylum in Kensington Market. Mina came to my place a few days later, putting it on and looking at her trim figure in my floor-length mirror. "Fits me to a T, perfectly, darling!" she smiled, pushing her firm boobs up with her hands, turning a bit to get a second look. I eyed her silver navel ring from an angle. My heart jumped.

Then one night she stayed over because of a sudden ice storm. We were all nearly paralyzed, living without any power, just using candles. I was surprised she didn't want to sleep on my second futon bed. It was already late and she turned away from me, taking her nylon nude bra off effortlessly under her T-shirt. She undid her shiny hair teasingly. Her embroidered leather pants came down over her firm legs and showed her smooth olive bum. Mina climbed into my bed comfortably. "You want this side?" I asked her, but she was content to stay put. There was a long silence as we both occupied the outer extremes of my futon, its hardness not giving way at all to our lonesome bodies. I turned around and snuggled up closer–closer. No gesture from her of resistance. I first held her slim body from behind, feeling her smooth curves, even began stroking her fine, jet-black hair. My warm breath was upon her; first her neck, then playfully on her ears as I bit, even lightly licked them. Oohs and aahs came out from her mouth. The place was like an ice-box, and we could hear the whir of tractors outside as they scraped the pavement and streets. After several minutes, I got brave enough to cup my hand over one of her petite round breasts, under her soft shirt. She didn't seem to mind. Small hands gently found mine as I did this. The heat from our bodies now made me kick my side of the blankets off a bit. It seemed only natural to peel off my crinkled T-shirt. Minutes later she decided to do the same, quietly. I could make out the beautiful slope of her breasts in the near darkness even though she kept her back towards me. We snuggled again. I rubbed up closer to her and became aroused. A secret wish that had come true. My hardness moving against her with small thrusts was a delicate gesture, beautiful and poetic. "You want to?...You feel so good...I've always liked you Min," I whispered in her ear. "Ssshh," she replied. I knew she was also liking our togetherness, but I didn't mean to have sex with her–only. She turned to face me. Her small soft hands travelled down and glided gently over my bum as she dug her nails into my taut upper legs, clawing me. *Did she mean it or was she merely playing with me?*

One hand came around my front and found my penis, was greeted by its stickiness. A bit of laughter from her, then me. My index finger rested on the front of her wet briefs. She took her hand slowly down her torso, leading mine in an arrow, pointing to the petalled place that gave her pleasure, radiance. It became a wombdance of a kind I had not discovered or felt for some time. Mina guided me–my fingers in, first one then two, with ease underneath what felt like a mesh thong (she had a liking for these). Her breathing intensified, and I could feel her chest rising and falling more quickly with each of our movements. She now wanted to lie on top of me, her moistness needing nourishment. As she moved up and down, my exposed shaft rubbed close to her, but not inside. I was content to hold onto the smooth smoothness of her hips, to feel her softness and rounded curves as my heart pounded. *How similar one felt with a man or a woman.* I pulled her back down. Placing my lips on hers, I began moving slowly on her, feeling the sensual burning of the smallness of her breasts rub against my shaven chest. The hard but soft caresses. Our heated closeness. Heartbeats pounding, echoing.

Beneath the warmth of the blankets, I travelled down, licking the middle part between her chest, gently biting and pulling on both rounded nipples, upright now, with my incisors, and continued still, past the deep gully of her navel that hid spices too exquisiste to detail and the hairs just below, putting my head between the valley that gave life. She adjusted the opening wider, allowing more of me in her, guiding me in deeper, deeper, steadying me with her petite hands and raising her thrusting hips. Heavy silence. Soft melodious words followed. "Ohh...there, there," she breathed quietly, amorously. She peaked in endless valleys and waves. Her rythyms became one incredible dance. The unquenchable wetness–tasteless but inviting.

I snuggled up against her minutes later. We shared a small kiss. Then another. It had been some time since I'd held a woman this way. "I'd secretly wanted you to sleep over Min...for us to do this, be *with* each other." But she was already asleep. Our breathing became one as I pulled the covers over us while still holding on to her tiny heated frame. The cold ice winds whirred outside. My first boyfriend's ancient angora blanket kept our bodies entwined, warm, against one another. We grew like a double cherry overnight.

my black "queer" body

As I came out from my shower, still towelling the beads of moisture off of my body, I looked at my self in my full-length mirror. At thirty-seven–an age which some gay men might argue was over the hill–my body had undergone a few changes that even I had begun to notice. My once firm stubbled pecs were now softer to the touch. My deltoids and chest had once been developed, much due to rigorous swimming. But what of my triceps and biceps? With various reps of curls, I'd pump up one night, only to lose it during the week! And my lats and obliques developed slowly, too slowly for what I could observe. I had to admit I had a bit of Daddy's face and Mummy's hands: the latter were delicate, small and I thought those of a cello player. There were my thin long fingers with rounded short nails I bit, much to my embarassment. On my right hand the index finger still couldn't bend properly because of a football mishap in high school in which it snapped back, never fully to recover, as I tried to catch the ball in the cold frigid air.

I always had a bit of a tummy–hidden under baggy T-shirts–and now it too became more worrisome. I'd look at it in various poses, only to finally accept it and my love handles. Crunches of course had not reduced it, but only running on a treadmill. Even then I never ran as much as I did step workouts, which a number of other men had also taken to. My pants were baggy, but during the wintertime a number of us would put on weight in the mid-section. Maybe this was just a natural thing that developed: bodies required heavier foods, storing it in places that basically bulged if fats were not burned off right away. People hibernated, slept more in the cold winter months in Canada, only to take flight briefly during our short hot summers.

From a side angle, my tan line was still there–dark brown suddenly met the lightness of my rounded ass. My most prized possession sat there somewhat limp, grounded by well-developed, dark, hairy, but firm quads and hamstrings. But my calves had always been small (was this the African in me?) even though I had run nearly daily throughout my high school and university days. Free standing squats for my legs were given up because of a lower back injury, and I started to use a squat machine only. My tight short brown pubic hair had always been kept to a minimum, and my weekly shaving of my chest, underarms, testicles, and now even anus had become nearly ritualistic, to the point if I didn't do it, I thought I had missed out on something. Isaac loved my chest hair, but I had given it up entirely. Rivers of red hot blood and white foam would mix together, running into each other as I took my sharp blade and scraped it gently up and down my body, usually on Thursday nights. I had to be extra careful when shaving the hair around my overly-sensitive nipples and penny-sized aeroles as well as underneath, between the testicles and anus, and the base of the penis. Shaving my body was always associated with getting ready for swimming, or going for my jaunts to the baths. A ritual, an escape of sorts.

Frantz Fanon wrote about the black body in incredible light of how it was defined in Western society. "There are times when the black man is locked into his body," he evinced. One could not escape the fact that our bodies had brought fear and uncertainty into white minds: to Them, we were sexual beasts, unclean, dirty, criminal, dark, alien. We were defined solely by our race and colour and looked upon as the "other." Black women, like men, were seen as highly sexual, thus continuing the myth that black mothers were unfit. I couldn't help but notice that my body was light-skinned, not dark, my hair straight and not kinky (although at fifteen, I could still remember the waves of crinkly hair as it bunched over my ears), my eyes Asian looking and slanted, and my average-sized cock, segmented into a dark brown and light brown. And that probably brought somewhat different connotations about how I might be categorized, even (mis)treated. For the darker our skins, the more cruel the judgement. The world's history has shown this to be true, and so have our interpersonal relationships. This was much the case as I went to meetings of AYA–a black gay and bisexual men's group. How would my brothers see me? Would they understand my plight in attempting to understand my self, or would they merely brush off my coming to the meeting as playful and a way to meet other black men with big dicks?

As I became more involved in AYA, I became aware of how different and racially "unidentifiable"–nearly invisible and God forbid, passable–I might seem to people; not Asian or black looking. *So who was I then?* The "rice queen" or "chocolate queen" would be too confused by my look(s). But I wanted neither, not their desirous and racist stares. I was black, felt black, only lighter. I just wanted to *be*, but given the way white gay culture perceived us and made us feel boxed in, catering to its stringent rules of *white* "beauty" and "desire," it was really impossible for us to feel free of these constraining categories that "queer" people of colour faced daily. Nor could we talk openly about our bisexuality. In the summer, with my dark tan, I was "Brazilian," or maybe "Spanish"; in the cold winter months, I might have been from Malaysia. Maybe only French-Canadian men wanted me, or my black gay and bisexual brothers. Frequently, we–the light-skinned ones–were seen to be the most desirable, but also the most *dangerous*–because we repre- sented the unimaginable: race-mixing, and a reminder of "racial and sexual defilement." Apartheid's lost children. *But did my brothers want to be me subconsciously?* Light- skinned? *Did I want to be them?* Dark-skinned, identifiable and once and for blaady all–*visible*.

My coloured family's history, the scar of apartheid, always remained somewhat ingrained. I now began to face my own internalized racism. "You've never had a black boyfriend," my best friend kept reminding me. "I am a threat to them. *But, I am not white. I do not think white.* It always shows through," I'd reply. My first boyfriend was Tonga-Hawaiian and white Australian. He looked Asian, but identified with his whiteness and upper-classness. Subconsciously, I might have feared loving darker-skinned men (was I fearing only my self, though?) but I had many black friends, both gay and straight. At the clubs I talked and danced with my brothers, hugged them. I had dates with other black men a few times, but they hadn't worked out. At the same time, I felt that I didn't want to be with a white man, for who could really trust them? And if there were only Asian men available, most wanted to meet white men who did not question who they really were, but accepted them as "white," not differently as I thought of my self, my racial identity. They didn't want to be othered and most never thought that deeply about how white gay culture still oppressed and exoticized them. No wonder I was so boyfriendless. Alone.

My chestnut brown body had no tribal marks, no piercings anywhere or scarifications, save for my forehead. That cross-like feature–nearly religious in its shape–was noticeable to me only if strangers looked at me closely in the light of day and pointed it out.

"What's that?" they'd ask. My eldest sister had chased me as a child into the sharp end of a door in our house in South Africa, but the stitches remained. Like the Sonjo, I had this "tribal" scar, a ntemi. The San, at the end of a puberty rite, would scar boys with a vertical line that ran down the middle of their forehead. They were then given a Choma haircut. This was part of the traditions of !Kung society. Scarification was a way Africans united their community, both the living and the dead. These marks said: "*I am because we are, and since we are, therefore I am.*" My eyes were small, and the crow's feet around them more noticeable. Brown pupils lit up whenever they were excited. The nose, flat and wide. The lips, full, round and sensuous. I had that small noticeable space between my incisors: a family trait, if anything else. My small ears still stuck out. And my dark brown head of hair was clipped just as my back hair in the Church-Wellesley village.

Like most men, I had gone to the gym. Years ago, I would be there for two hours daily, working with weights diligently, but lately I was drawn to the water. My body was toned, even beautiful, I thought. It was Yukio Mishima, the famous Japanese gay novelist, who said that "when at last I came to own a beautiful body I wanted to show it off like a child. But the body is doomed to decay. I for one will not accept such a doom." He committed ritual seppuka suicide (for him to this was the "ultimate maturbation"), disembowelling himself, followed by the suicide of his young lover, over a "nationalist cause." Like many men, I worked my body, hoping that it would not fail me. But over the last few years, I had felt as though there was little I could do about aging and fighting against it. I was tired of seeking the *perfect* body, and felt it was time to do something else. My body—with all of its imperfections—had no longer become such an important thing of beauty to work on, and I had sought spiritual fulfilment in my writing that would in turn affect how my mind would function, and I suppose, ultimately affect the thing that encircled me, too. But sitting down writing for long periods had its effects on posture, too! I would always have my marvelous mind, I thought, despite the slow death of my flesh and muscle. The body was only a temporary vessel. Yet too few of us realized this.

We black men who were gay had learned to celebrate our bodies. We had otherwise been looked at as dangerous and exotic. Black bodies were once enslaved, whipped, hung, burned and brutalized—especially the penis—the uncontrollable, thick, long part of us that dictated and controlled us, and was an instrument feared and extolled by white men and women. We were very much sexualized, fetishized and dehumanized and had to live with these deep emotional and psychic wounds. Mapplethorpe's photography showed us—our penises primarly—as ponderous and dangerous. *Man in Polyster Suit* of 1980, with a brilliant use of whites, greys and blacks, illustrated a man clad from shoulders to knees only in a suit. A large flaccid penis hung aesthetically out of the unzipped fly of the pants, with a piece of white shirt hanging out, exposing the phallus's dark hue. The powerful penis was celebrated, flaccid, limp, hard, erect—but *we* were not. The white gay artist, overly "obsessed with beauty," had made his point: black men had risen so far economically, but they still had sexual prowess as their only bargaining tool. And white gay men bought into this idea and so, too, we. The black man as stud without economic power, still a boy in the master's house. It was Fanon, after discussing the racial fantasies of his white psychiatric patients, who wrote: "One is no longer aware of the Negro, but only of a penis: the Negro is eclipsed. He is turned into a penis. He *is* the penis." The white gay man was disempowered and driven to obsession by this "overpowering sexual animal" with its brute strength but devoid of will. Too often I had seen advertisements in *Xtra!* in Toronto, Ottawa and Vancouver, attempting to convey the very same message to its mostly white gay readership without question.

Whereas black and gay and bisexual men are engorged penises, Asian men are thought to be passive, submissive, not even pleasurable. They are "houseboys," "bottoms." They and we are all forced to compare ourselves to *Xtra!* or the *Advocate*'s definition of beauty: white, male, middle class, muscled. All too often, on the Internet and elsewhere, I have seen too many Asian men ask for the same thing, predictably: a *single white man*, only! Toronto has North America's second-largest Chinese community, and writer-filmmaker Richard Fung has said that the gay ghetto has been "a site of racial, cultural and sexual alienation sometimes more pronounced than that in straight society." I would argue that this is indeed true. Men look for status. And in gay society, status is equated with white European looks, social and economic position, education, age or youth and sexual prowess. My Asian friend from Hong Kong told me about how other Asian men viewed him: "Asian men look at me as if I am the type to date only white gay men. *Not typically Asian*. They reject me automatically until they find out I like men like them," he said. As if Asian men could not desire each other.

And what of Latino men? There are differences according to which group we are talking about. Brazilians do not see themselves as Mexicans, and Central Americans are seen as an underclass. My Chilean friend told me, "White men don't understand being together. We are supposed to be partners, lovers. We want to do everything together, all of the time. But it seems like we only connect in bed. Most gay people are lonely. They have an internal conflict: you want your own space but also you are crying out for company–and love. It's unresolved. I see it when I go to the bathhouse. They want someone to hold them. Someone to talk to them. Not me, though. We don't understand the *open* relationship," he continued on in what seemed like a long, articulate soliloquy. "I give you my heart, my soul and body, everything too. It's too hard to understand. Three days later, I see you fucking someone else. Sex is available. It's fast. White gay men have sex like they drink coffee. What is scary is now I'm starting to feel the same way after being here for years. I'm like them because I'm attracted to white guys, blue eyes, yes–fucking blonds!" He had just broken up with a man.

"Part of the problem is we don't speak the language properly. Communication is poor. The Canadians expect you to adopt the way they think," I also heard. "You are a foreigner who comes here. My partners have never asked me about my culture, *my* Chile. To survive, you have to keep your morals or you are condemned to live in this ghetto for the rest of your life," he said, his voice cracking. His words also made me think of my relationships years ago, even now. I too wanted to be with my boyfriends and tell them of my culture.

The black community doesn't understand what being gay is, and the gay community doesn't understand what being black is. The black community is concerned with hetero-sexism–marriage and family values–while the gay community in Canada is concerned with "coming out," which works against these norms, both socially and religiously. *Xtra!*,

Toronto's gay magazine, is *too* queer for a black brother to take home to show to his family. Telling my sisters I was "gay" was no easy task, and I did so only five years after first going to the white gay clubs, which gave me some sense of community. But we never did discuss our "blackness" in our coloured family: we got these feelings, intuitions and understandings from our parents. *We were unmothered yet othered.* We did identify with racism, but when it came to identifying ourselves racially, we could not name who we were except to say that we were mixed or still "coloured." Racism still persisted in our family: one sister married a white man and he was easily accepted into the family, while the other one married a black man, and he was not.

Only after I had had a long-term relationship did I tell my sisters about my self. And this was most difficult. Homophobia exists in coloured families in South Africa. My relatives there would think that only white people would get involved with this sort of thing. Reclaiming my name as a moffie (the derogatory term, a variation of "hermaphro-dite," has been associated with Cape coloured community but it also means "male homo-sexual," "effiminate male" and "transvestite.") is a powerful thing to do: for it says that I am proud of being South African, of a man loving men, of reclaiming my silenced desire that is still ever changing, still *becoming.*

But volunteering in white gay organizations oppressed me deeply. They still had not come to terms with the fact that minority "queers" needed to see themselves reflected in the community. It was only after joining AYA that I felt some sort of welcome. However, because I looked more light-skinned, I felt a certain amount of silencing going on. My work on the board proved fruitful in the end. For once I felt I had finally found my place working in an organization that was committed to fighting against racism and heterosex-ism. It was the *blackness*, the never-ending commotion of laughter and joy of greeting and meeting other black gay and bisexual men when there were so few safe spaces in the community for us to gather. We never did discuss how class issues affected us all. Black Caribbean middle-class gay and bisexual men ran it. We were vocal about showing our presence in black community events in the city and also voiced changing the stereotypical images the white gay community had of us. Black men wanted to socialize, say "Hi girl–what's up?", see if we could find a new friend or date, as much as talk politics. We did all! There were AYA fashion shows (who could forget them, or Michelle Ross doing her thing at the Y?), poets jammin' and our bright tropical Pride booth on Church Street.

In the final end, I would suggest that black, Asian and Latino men have been culturally fetishized by white men and conversely we have fed into these false notions to the point that we have been "forced" to leave our culture behind. We still need our families for affirmation of *who* we are racially, even if our families bring us pain. At the same time, black men, according to Cornel West, may have consciously desired and even played with the white gaze of fascination, of "exoticizing." He recognized this as he interviewed Bill T. Jones, the famous African-American dancer-choreographer, for he had also agreed to be photographed by Mapplethorpe, as long as the latter would not photograph his "dick." Subconsciously, then–did the snow queen exist in all of us? Or maybe were *we* just too afraid to admit it?

am i blk enuf for u?

i am nearlee as
fair skinned
as my distant mudah who criies 4 mee
i existtt outsiide
yr wurld, but what ees it, cuz i can't paint it, can't putt my fingah on itt
brotha, my wurds don't come out right   i's ain't even dark brown
save for blisterin summahs
not eeven inklike–as da
stufff i's weeeve, speeek
but i's kissss
yr marbble ebbonee
cheeeks, each 1
huggg u tite, my thing rubbbin u, so wee are 1–alwaysss
stilll unsure
of what u
think of mee
my lonelee brotha, lonelee like nina singing, moaning da blues
your tuff skinnn
exposed ta their
hideuss remarkkss
even da piece of paper u
ran ta get like a nigga at da white mahn's school
means nothin
to da boys
means nothin
to da boys
the b-boy clothes r yr suittt n tttie
laughin out, we know mammma knows chile, mammma knows chile
and i sayys to u one ddday
in dat dark bar where dah ghost mahns frequent on sun-days
where deyys
only wear kool white undahwear without a care, us 2
holdin hands playfullee, in hour-long shaddowws, in hour-long shaddowws
i's tink dat only sistahs
want u, only sistahs
yr eeyes, sad, cried like a long histry lesson–malcolm, marley, mandela
u agreed–and dat wuz yr pas, dat is de fact of life, not liees chile
honee, we both in/visible ta dem mahns
dancin like two *free* negroes lone, swayin lone
as smoke risin, swirlin, trappped in herre   chokin
dancin like two *free* negroes lone, swayin lone

hear meee brotha

sof han takes waves
into steamd shinee ebonee face
feel it, feel da wintry waddah
rush through u
up
    down
da wavy un-clear waddah
to afrika   rise   rise   rise
to afrika   home
he sits to kool, replenishhh
sits 2 feeel
looks dis way, dis way   brotha
du u feel it?
is da wadduh da blud of life? da muddah?
at da beach
dem old naked men–colurrd in/visible, wrinkled by boooze n smoke from dem dark
bars
walk round proudlee, gazin at brown, ebony bodeees, dark
as cold as da lan
yr long braids of histree–once stolen–now washd
yr long braids of time–now regained–now washd ashore
by waddahs dat killd da fish, dat saw da indiun blud spill, sizzul
listun, listun
to da muddah/land
in da distunce
islan daze, brotha
jah people calll u, jah people calll u
but do u hear em, brotha?
do u as u
wait n wade in da waddah, look for cluuus, search for your reeflection?
da dancin tide
beats to da rhytmmm of yr sorrowful shore
everywhere u look da white light blinds u
we so lone, brotha/luv is like dat, nigga
a sickness dat don go way
c.n. tower over us–dis is kanada, dis is land of da white mahn
da koolness washes da thing theys wan so bad brotha
and standin firm, u take it, risin in your heavy-hearted hand
smilin, beatin it, fas, fasttter, heart poundz like a-frika explodin,
like kingston still in flamz
where u member seein a batty mahn's bodee washh up on a beach in port royal,
blud all over him
where u member seein a batty mahn's bodee washh up on a beach in port royal,
blud all over him

goin to meeet da mahn

da mahn says eee's gotttta teeech uddahs
gotttta teeech and preeech ta uddahs ta du da thing eee luvs, dusss so well
angriest nigger in da country
ta take up his hahn

stumbled cross da mahn at wellesley sub-way dress in ol jeeens
waitin for somebody, eyys lookin roun n roun to da streeet
honee, i's walked passsed im, still eyyin who he was/is
and when i saw da mahn sittin or walkin, jivin with his sisterly brotha, i's says hellllo
da mahn's eyys gestured ta meee politeleee
should av memberd ta say "u da big brotha now, u da prophet now!"

da sisterly brotha sung, "He's comin here more often–da mahn gotta live!"
i's memberd eyyin im shoppin for wurds, ideeas heeer
wurds to learn, wurds, forgotten unknown storeees n tunes–not miles, not parker
maybe bessie, billie   honeee u silleee
and i says–is da mahn 1 a us?
and der was jus a smile, a brief smile wid wiidde wiidde eyys
frum a brotha dat doo da shufffle in da darrk, lonesome eyys
im got big wurds, BIGGAH dan da mahn

las night i was in da village, walkin as i do like uddah nights, nights when
shirts is off, when eyys don blink but stare at pumpppped hungree bodees
da mahn outsiide, sittin niclee at dah beestro where no 1 eeets
pigs' tails n tings ain't on da menu
im wid a prettteee white ladeee frien, younga, like is daughtah

i wavd to im, jus beginnin to mouth is firs name
only to seee im turn is grey head a storeees n pain, as if to loook at dah
white emptee wall
my heart didn't know whad ta say cept dat i might not beee a brotha to da mahn
as if dis wurd mahn were a street nigga, as if dis wurd mahn were a street nigga
"is seecret still deeep in im, waitin for wurds to cum out"
deep in im like a chil waitin ta beee born
im no want meee for companeee
whyl da mahn's ladee frien listendd, ate quietleee
sippin chattin sippin chattin

guess da mahn didnt wan dis brotha jivin, laughin wid em
pardonnn moah   huh!!
too fraid what peepul might say, theenk
afters allll griots mus stilll get spect n' pay

78

underground

I.

They looked
at him
like he
was a nigga
and he
fucked Them
over and
over again
in his
mind
until it hurt.

II.

why can't u be u   h
step, reach, arms up swayin, move, eyes closed. breathe
why can't u be u   o
step, reach, arms up swayin, move, eyes closed. breathe
why can't   l
step, reach, up
u be   d
step, reach, up
u
reach   m
u
reach...u?   e

III.

"i'm a *mad* fuckin' woman. don't mess with me now!" stephanie yells, as she struts
her stuff and big ass in her too-tight red velvet catsuit on stage at the red spot. we
laugh so hard it hurts while she continues to read the audience. "oh i don't like small
cocks, you know c-o-c-k-s, as the whites say, but long, long ding-dongs!" more
outbursts from us, and the brothers slap themselves silly. this is american thanksgiv-
ing and the yanks are in town: "yeah i want you to *give* honey," she goes on, "and
then i'll receive. check your guns at the door, chile–cause we don't do that kinna stuff
here!" we howl. now she belts out her aretha, tina, jennifer, and diana–and the house
comes down, while black cat keeps spinning his jumpin' tunes, and the "talent show"
starts late–again. "talent" could be some scar-bo-rough-o kid posing in funky platforms that gladys wore with a tight silver mini to the usual faded white queen having
no "voice" or rhythm.

for b. at 35

you are the youngest and only son of four, really the eldest most honoured son, but your secret is mine–not your age. your search for men and weekly dinners you have with your auntie where you play mah-jong later makes you giggle with chinese tea in between while you laugh a deep belly laugh yet you remain quiet about your older cousin from vancouver who lavishes himself with expensive jewelry. he is a good son to his mother who cannot afford much.

your parents are not privy to your ghettoized world where older white men who want to compare bank accounts and unbending penises desire to touch your soft smooth skin and jelled black hair only for you to shrug them off–always. you think of your last trip to hong kong where you were surrounded by men like you who desired you as a red lotus. the harbour that overlooked your friend's expensive condominium in the mountains and staffed by maids appealed to you, but you knew you were just an invited guest.

the warm breeze that came to you from your country, licked your meloncholy away so much that it loved you, loved you, knowing that within two years it would engulf you forever and your life would be here–not this cold white country–because no one ever came up to you in crowded subways to bump into you who looked like you, who looked so good dressed in the latest western styles, looked so confident of yourself even though you were only a visitor in a land you once called home, a united but distant land where many feel the blue sky of the west should be painted even more beautifully as the yellow sky of the east.

the crisis of the poet

we speak loudest when
countries are at war
and families are ripped apart
even when our own lovers
leave
tears can scar
and wounds can not heal
they only remind us
that the child who lies sleepless at night because her stomach aches, cries out
becomes our concern   our sister, brother
that is our crisis
and the time when america killed hussein's men
and the time when america raped grenada
and the time when america did nothing for people with aids
and the time when america fucked the people of nicaragua
and the time when it silenced allende   forever
and the time when a white south african imagined that they were *victims* and won
another booker
but we cheered wildly in the streets of santiago, london and madrid with signs of
pinochet perdió
dripping with our blood, the blood of los desaparecidos held high above our heads
but we cried when riel was hung and manitoba is now the biggest penitentiary of his
people in this land–and canada is a *free* country
writing is *our* revolution
not the gun
we can't stop just because wars stop
we can't stop just because welfare moms get an extra ten dollars a week
and get that job on the factory floor, coming home on the subway
asleep, their breasts too tired to feed their young
and because a sister who is raped over and over again finally gets the man in jail
and because an old woman you know gets out of queen street
is "set free"   on the street, debilatingly
standing at a corner, asking us for money
her desperate eyes like the ones i saw in mummy, people staring
like the ones i saw on the streets of vallarta, chicago and cancun
we continue the cause
not because we have to
but because we must
because that is our duty
our destiny

What's Wrong with Jack Lewis's film *Dragging at the Roots*

(Letter to the Editor, Xtra, Toronto)

May 28, 1999

Jack Lewis's film *Dragging at the Roots* at the Inside Out Festival raised various concerns among coloured and black Canadian South Africans who viewed it. As a reviewer of the program of South African films for *Xtra!*, and looking at the film a second time, I felt that it was an inaccurate portrayal of what really happened in District Six regarding the immense poverty, disillusionment and finally the horrific forced removal of coloured families from the area enshrined through the apartheid legislation of the 1960s.

Kewpie, the moffie (drag queen) narrator, tells us of her romantic notions of the place, thus erasing what actually happened to those who lived and faced harassment in District Six. This white gay interpretation misrepresents the true extent of human suffering and misery. The fact that a liberal white filmmaker could boldly claim that "the coloured people are my people" as justification for him to make a film on our experiences is a further attempt to rob us of our identity and nationalism–still. Lewis, in defence, claimed that the film was not meant to be shown outside of South Africa and that he would edit its contents to include new material about apartheid's legacy. "Oh, ja," he insisted to me, "there was a coloured moffie I know who told me that he and his chums threw a party just as the police came, and before the bulldozing was to take place, they set the house on fire!" But why not then include this in the film? *It is through the lens of white colonialist power, via apartheid, that we view the film.* We laugh at ourselves on the screen only because we have no other power but to view our subordinated lives. This kind of mentality–to "other" the "other"–still pervades in the minds of white South Africans who still largely control and have ready access to the media there. And it is that media that has not been reformed to define who *we* really are, because those who control it still define, subordinate and continue to dominate us.

The Inside Out Festival failed *miserably* to reach out to our community when it decided to screen Lewis's work, here. A white businessman was the sole person to identify himself in supporting the film and in "bringing it to Canada." Hence, the main audience of the film was to be *white*, not non-white. Finally, I told Lewis directly that we need to hear our own stories, and I sincerely hope that Inside Out is currently working with coloured and black South Africans in making films that showcase our unique lives and experiences.

A new festival seeks this kind of inclusiveness and a more thoughtful critique of identity politics.

82

walking on yonge

i see a lone man talking to himself, clothes so worn
as old as he
as old as she
that you want to turn the other way
just pretend to look in front of you
just pretend to look in front of you
see the beautiful puffy dreamy flakes
as they land on your warm nose, face, hit the shimmering ground
smile   smile
you catch a glimpse of his lonesome figure
while shoppers are too busy to notice
he now crouches on the white salted street, against
the wall of some
cheap lingerie store
where women with little money
buy something sexy to make
their pot-bellied husbands happy
his ears rest hard
as the traffic and city
scream at him
all day and night
to fit, conform
his life is poetry and you don't even see it
he is your lost brother, uncle, father, son

*for Toronto's homeless—a national crisis which the federal, provincial and municipal
governments refuse to acknowledge*

revenge of the squeegees

i fill my bucket with beautiful scummy water as if it's my new briefcase like
me goin to work on bay for forty bills a day enuf for
cigs, beer, and a big break/fast
july 16, sixteen of us rrested
even a woman
with a squeegee
pasted on
her backpac
friggin cops
want us
the fuck
out, call
us urban
guerillas
no business
license, says
the fuckin
province
no taxes to
worry bout
fuck welfare
fuck harris
fuck the fairy
tale wedding
and white
picket fence,
house, too
we keep washin
angry winshels
on col corners
here, there
squeegees
we stay
blackened on
fiery streets,
reclaim them,
forever free
forever strong.

the people do not mourn him

she

saultered across the manicured lawn, running stomach   empty as usual

wearin hand-me downs, running shoes stolen from bi-way, unlaced

eyes   aflame

catching sight of a man sleeping, silently, breathlessly

death can be so ugly and beautiful   it makes all of us want to take polaroids

he lays there, on that golf course   hole 18   his last

blood drips   BLOOD DRIPS   drowsily onto the sea green green

his LIPS lie lifelessly   thin lips

which uttered 1,000 useless rehearsed speeches   hand signing documents shakily

stolen lives

the television blared UNIONS ARE TO BLAME

what's that mean, momma?

her father died, died in that emergency ward,   her mother's boyfriend told to leave

"you're defrauding the government," the worker said

she could beg with her sad puppy face   where they now lived

on sorry shuter street in that shelter where women walked fast on dark streets

with cranky kids screamin, holerin   stale SMOKE stuffing the air of their room

you stay way from them hookers on the STREET   momma says

she looks round, sees no one, takes the man's golf club, bright white ball, a dewdrop of

blood painted on it   skips, skips   HOME

petals weep but the rose lives eternally

The java sea holds silent secrets
petals weep but the rose lives eternally
brown brown fidgeting hands on his leather bound bible
neck covered with scars of his people
that remembered the history of our
demise and struggle
bodies disappearing   disappearing bodies
their secrets will soon speak
as indonesian spies keep watch
even i cannot kiss the statue of jesus
built by bloody hands, suharto's army
blood drips over that white deathly statue
blood of blood of blood on outstretched weary hands
pointing to the pale green sea
freedom? what freedom?
first the portuguese, then indonesia's dogs
worse than cambodia our lips say
women sterilized by doctors who laugh loudly

dili now in flames, dili where our parents lived
crumbled as our men are separated forever? from
their wives, children, from their tongues, limbs
papaya leaves and root vegetables become our rice
our bishop who prayed for newly found peace,
his house raised to the ground as the world blinked
kijangs running around picking us up, eyes in terror
machetes of the militiamen mimick the crop harvest
bodies cut down like cheap ripe bananas
angry violent mouths want to eat peaceful hearts
the grim hover of helicopters, helicopters
sold to the indonesian military
bloody bras, sanitary napkins, underpants on the
church's silent ghostly steps
a rose grows, cries out at santa cruz cemetery
guns silencing weeping
funeral marchers, our relatives, our people
a silent prayer, many sung hymns remind us
petals weep but the rose of freedom
remembers, remembers, lives eternally, peacefully.

86

what defines us	where our future lies

what defines us

paternal control
"do you have airmiles?"
team work, teams, policies
the excruciating buzz of cell-phones
Y2K, *e* this, *e* that
globalization

technology, the pharmaceutical
mind-set and cloning
the privatization of our health

always running for the bus

watching the clock
government cutbacks, "efficiencies"
privatization; capitalism

24 floors up with no view
anger, brutal anger, violence
helplessness, homelessness
powerlessness
sex, money, greed
mutual funds for the kids' education
the angry erect phallus
death/loss of culture
western imperialism, christianity
the iron fist, sjambok, the gun

gay apartheid

white is right, might

the masochistic, cyber 90s
u.s. military industrial complex

"it takes a village..."
the crush of hard metal over the earth

the lonely incarcerated individual

where our future lies

mummy, i missed you
i just spoke to a homeless woman
god, that woman's poetry changed my life
the sign on the beach said "turn them off"
together, we watched as we lit a candle for our place
that homeless indian woman whose relatives are
slaves, is my mother–she is the earth's child

i want to make you dinner tonight, okay? just us 2
the laid-off nurses were asked to come back but they
all went to african villages helping those with aids
everyone striked against the transit authority
and played with friends that sunny day
i want to live and laugh and grow a garden
i know, the demonstration on the streets is at 2 p.m.
a guy named marx had some noble ideas mr.
president
chi, the flow of energy that gives life, empowers me
i'm not too good at hugging, but here's a long one
let me help you find a home, don't worry...
in the self-help section she found herself for a year
she sold her jewelry and gave the money to a shelter
dady wuz pleesed cuz he gve me a bk to read
her delicate fingers made the sign of the yoni
i want to keep my parents old things, and learn zulu
muhammad said things to us, to our slave mothers
we joined hands, forming a circle, then wrote a
letter of love and community to the government
he left the ghetto and built a home, relearning
forgotten wor(l)ds
honey, thing is–black is beautiful–afros are back!
and the spics, chinks and red brothers are in power
i can't get enuf of barry white and those platforms!
flowers bloomed where blood was shed, and the sun
told us war was over: it joyously said it in africa,
asia, the caribbean and latin america
how come when a sistah says this no one listens?
my body hugged the green grass, the trees spoke to
me and afforded shade that cooled my thoughts
prisons were closed and those jailed would get a
free education and a decent job

flowers have memory

88

puerto vallarta waves

she came plunging at us
the pulvarizing push of waves, sand, stone
all of her natural
beating beauty, against us, against the soft shore
throwing us back like juegos infantiles as we dove in
her rocking, swooshing voice
more captivating
than any stormy woman
i've known
sucking us into her strong
arms   mouth
the sweet salty smell and taste
of her liquid breath
of her ice-cold touch
sun stroking smooth bodies, unclothed
on her soft bellied shore
bright sun touching
hot bronzed brown surfaces
the cool breeze licking us
encircling us
black birds   pelicans
glide above like marauding vultures
reminding us that
man and nature are one, but she
dominates, despite our attempt
to prevent her from speaking furiously
the succulent violent waters
her plunge, her last words sprayed
her salty breath, urgent call
and tongue lashes of sand forcefully tumble to shore
leaving a reminder of that night
i discovered you, desired you
that perfect puerto vallarta night
and thought about (my) life
my only words to you: i can taste the sea on you...
asking my self
who you were–the fatherless aztec
who am i
the landless, motherless african
my heart silently speaking, exploding
finally, endlessly, wordlessly

...sí, sí

my open bruised heart
mistook him
or did it?
for love, sí
for i loved him, adored him, sí
for i kissed and enveloped him, sí
sharing laughs, smile after smile
for i bit his sweet red strawberry lips, ears, nose, leaving love-bites, sí
for he jerked away, laughed and his dark hazel eyes lit up so
when i did this, sí
for i scribbled poem after poem in our sweat
each one made me live and die
about him, about his country and people, sí
for i felt we had lived together,
in his padre's large empty house in tepic
in my cheap penthouse apartment in the old crowded town
that overlooked the pacific ocean, sí
for we ate together and my knee
would always brush his underneath
the table, the cloth covering us, sí
for the tortillas de harina and freshly made salsa
with spicy chicken were what
we enjoyed most, sí
for my burning brown hand would always reach out for his, sí
for we slept and hurriedly got up to make out, sí
under starlit nights, sí
for we spoke and even though
my spanish was non-existent, and his english
wasn't much better
but i always used my
french
or we sat quietly, sí
but we didn't have to say much
to know what we felt, sí
and when we looked at the ocean, together
from high above, from high above on descanso del sol, just us two
out of view of the military police
with me holding him from close behind, sí
and the night, breathless, breathing before us
and the full moon, the stars, above us–they were shimmering like him, sí
and with me turning him around, sí

kissing his hot brown, brown hand
and looking into his soft staring frida kahlo eyes, sí
eyes so silent you wondered about him
and him telling me, "i am mucho happy, sí"
and me saying the same, sí, sí
i realized that there was not more to life than this, sí
and his silence then became my silence, sí
and the sea's silence became our silence,
and the thrashing of the waves
booming, booming crashes
brought us closer together, sí
and the day i left, walking back to my hotel
the bumpy cobblestone road leading the way
i pulled him into the backyard of a house in the old town
where we kissed one more final time, one long beautiful time, sí
first looking around to see if it was alright to do so
openly holding hands in the old taxi, the sweat floating off us, sí
our mouths especially silent–not able to utter any words
that would console us, sí
we noticed rosary beads and a small cross
on the mirror of that taxi, the driver an old man
who probably went to mass weekly
his weary eyes looked the other way,
with him muttering "maricón, maricón" underneath his breath
and at the airport, i took mi amor by my side hurriedly
and sat with him, to hold his gentle hand secretly
underneath a table in a far away corner
and finally waved as long as i could, sí
and he stayed there
and stood still, stood still, my heart of gold
my rememberance of innocent young love
now gracing his soft delicate brown neck, sí
our hearts crying out, crying out, sí
i had no idea that our separation
would be even more difficult
than the separation of a mother
and child, for i had known those
both, sí, for i had lived those both
god delivered him from the sea
lost love has no close friend
when i would ever see
him again, i did not know   sí, sí, sí

Pensée

We feel like two strangers, and lovers–oui, in a a foreign country. We do not know each other well but have a bit of trust and friendship–a familiarity between us that brings us together. But nothing, not even love, he thought was forever. Non. And so he journeys to a place called Montreal with me to see, learn, discover. And so he walks the one-way streets in cheap blue running shoes, wearing some of my clothes, but he makes by and uses his broken English and full knowledge of Spanish, yet does not understand the French Fact and the demands that the Québéçois place on foreign visitors, especially foreigners from other provinces. Bombs went off in mailboxes thirty years ago and they killed Laporte. "Just watch me!" Trudeau the sell-out barked, and he sent in the troops, smilingly but anxious. The white country was paralyzed. I am not a child of Trudeau, but a fucking traitor. And now I sit here, in this troubled torn land and think of life, knowing that I too am a lonely traveller, the deep green sea changing before me, the sun's strong hand on me and he is walking, sweating, walking, sweating. How will he find me, here? Will he see the same person he met and smiled at on Los Muertos Beach, or holding onto him as we walked arm in arm quietly in the darkness of the beach in Yelapa, one or two fires on the cool deep sand lighting our way back to our room, the mountain mist rising before us on its steep forested green slopes? I cannot place too many demands on him and he is his own person. I cannot control him as his path and destiny are predetermined. Like an endless ocean always moving, escaping, waves thrasing back and forth peacefully and forcefully, shores changing, waters tumbling to shore making gulps, storms approaching. And that path leads to a place I cannot see...

***

I don't like the smell of poverty. Like rotting garbage. Uh-uh. Too many fuckin young French Canadians on social assistance. Let them fuckin separate, I say. Let em go. You think I'm angry don't you? Hell they say, "Why don't you learn *our* language," and I say–look, I've been colonized by the fuckin British. Miss Thing ain't now gonna be fucked by the French. Naw sir...

untitled: 7. 6. 99

i looked at unclear pictures of zulu spears
at the tattoo parlour where you notice someone's
arm display whatever poem they have made their own
but it was the chinese sign for
the thing that i felt to visit, pull my body through
while hearing my mother's soft voice
where i would seek solace, take boyfriends to: how it
surprises me with its quiet, soft soothing trickle
the shiny blue-black stamp on my right tanned deltoid would be
inscribed on my writing arm, forever   like a beautiful proverb
this, as he looked at me grimace from the window outside
the shop in montreal near the graffitied walls of rue saint-dominique
as stephan the tattoo artist pierces the sharp steel needle deep deep inside
my bracing arm in his long leather chair   clenched teeth, fists
black ink spills like blood into puffy veins
east meets west
reminding me of his sunny face and cool stare
the time we first met
the brilliant fiery aztec sun, the half-finished sign on his lower back
just above the rise of his hard ass, a point towards him
and i came quietly noticing it and him
his soft silent beauty, his soft silent beauty
cool water, the fiery hot sun, my tattoo, his–us, sí, oui
blue-green ocean waves, the playful romantic beach, my tattoo, his–us, sí, oui
our symbols which sustain life
give our lives the same meaning
even the same pressing but unknown path
and i hold onto him
and my hand waits for him as we walk; he comes to me, me after him
running up from mile-high beaudry station
i am breathless for more words, oui
like two little boys
our lips collide like an endless field of flowers which xochipilli has given us
his padre named him after him
my vader name me after him
there is deep meaning in being named after the father
we are expected to carry on the family's traditions and look after our troubled sisters
and mothers
this, as we spoke high atop of a roof-top patio at la trac in the village–just like the
bustling barn
only darker, overlooking rue sainte-catherine where lone men in tank tops walk in
long shorts
with me holding onto him gently from behind, gently from behind
leaning into his tiny frame as if we are one, as if we are one

canción

my jagged cold hands bringing you to the concrete shore, the city lights beckoning you
cool licks of my sea-blue breeze
through your thin hot burning bodies
the young boy playing against the wind, trying to stand up, but unable to
the child's mother casually looking around, on him
your burnt hands embrace as they did when you walked the maple treed streets
my large cousin, the sea, at los muertos beach, like my cold
waters, spitting in your face, causing you to laugh, turn your head
as you cross my rough wet exposed skin
my damp breezes surrounding you, holding you, holding you
remember, remember
celebrate me as i do your yearning
celebrate me as i do your mourning
unescorted men cannot walk too close together
at night's edge along the malecón by the sea
where lovers always meet, swoon secretly
as the unsmiling police in white hats keep an eye on things
and jesus is carved out in white sand and lit by candles
but my swirling, swooshing breath
will always taste your young green love
will always visit my chilly warm body
where you ran like young niños, shoeless
putting up your mexican blanket, its lines of lively colour
exploding like new flower buds in yelapa
lying together, apart, naked, touching, the heat
dripping from brick brown backs
to hairy round asses, the feel, the touch of their bouncing beauty
and at the day's end, always folding your blanket neatly
looking into each other's smiling eyes
as my course sands, shaken, shaken off
licked you hard, eyes closed
eyes seeing only each other
in their reflection
in their quiet joy

corazón

do you whisper my tender name, softly
look, reach for the same besos, love bites
upon your cinnamon-brown neck, ears
into the still burning night
as you spill your sweet seed
over and over again and again
lips quivering for mine?
glowing dreams of green pastures: the train
runs as you listen to her soft voice, mine
i touch your soothing face,
dark eyes, round red cheeks,
hands, see you in the floor mirror,
my undraped legs splayed, shaven chest
heaving, four images of me, all craving, licking
you on my hard, hard bed–the very same one
that held our burnt bronzed frames
saw us move, float upon as our words blew by
the silky sea i imagine, await your sunny smile upon
señiorita, is the same one which brought us together and its
shores i cannot see always make room for one more blanket: ours.

of human truth and injustice

He had lived in la frontera along the U.S.-Mexico border, "making more money" than he did in Monterrey. But he was never happy there. The other took a trip to the old town in Mexico, and he took an interest in watching the men and women selling things–doughnuts, bright blankets, hats, and clothes–on the beach. He soon learned to say "no gracias." It was the sight of the limosneros on the bumpy streets, holding onto their babies and putting their rough brown hands out for money, that caught his eye in the late nights as he would go out to eat somewhere. Mummy came back to him, and so did his nearly poor homeless sisters. Even though there wasn't money, he'd send it to them or make a mild curry that lasted him a few days. In his student days his hands were those that shared burning the American flag, and like many others, he angrily signed petitions against the Free Trade deal.

His amigo's abuela lived quietly on a large farm in Chiapas and his padre owned property, including in Vallarta, close to the sea. He always yelled at those on the street washing windows of cars because he told me that they earned more than he and paid no taxes. Like Daddy, I owned nothing. I supposed having rented the penthouse in the old town would make me seem rich, and when his friend visited, the view before him, it produced that effect. "This is beautifu...l," he said silently, and I held him anxiouly as we both stared into the darkness of the sea before us, the crashes of high waves in the unknown distance. I wanted my burning brown arms to hold onto him as long as the sea tides flowed back and forth. Back and forth. Sí. We shared large red flowers of joy soon after.

One had gone to university, the other took a hair design course. One sculpted people's minds, the other, women's hair–women who always talked, told him of their trips abroad, of extravagant plans they had made for their daughters' marriages to professional men.

And they dined out at restaurants here and there in Vallarta and Montreal, enjoying a beautiful quiet moment, sipping twenty-eight dollar sangria overlooking the fashionable cafés on Rue Cresent after they gave way to the mid-day heat of the long bustling streets. But they did not speak of those who lived naked, huddled in puddles of urine and feces in Mexico's state asylums.

His amigo soon went for the blond-haired, blue-eyed gringo who would only end up casting his eyes, touching other men in the end.

96

attends-moi

8. 16. 99

It has nearly been a month since you left Toronto–and me. My birthday has just passed, and that too was a moment of joy that was filled with some anxiety. I am sitting here, writing from the very place you came to look out off my balcony, to see the city lights, listen to the roar of the traffic below. What did you see or imagine, mi amor? How beautiful the city can be at night? How different the clouds look here, because there are no mountains, or you can't see and bewonder the Cerro de la Silla? But I also remember telling you how ugly it was, living here, among the tall faceless buildings, as we ate our first dinner together in the warmness of the early evening. And I knew your distaste for living in highrises–like mine. But could you envision yourself staying here with me? Could you? Did that ever cross your mind, mi amor?

I could guess that your first impression of me was that I was not rich, even though I brought you to a rented penthouse that night in Vallarta, the sound and taste of the ocean breeze beyond us. And then, as we ate dinner on my balcony here, you asked me if I were the same person you met in Mexico. And I said "sí," telling you that I have not lost the sense of what I desired to do with my life. That my writing would take me places. You told me that you still wanted to discover the world, making me feel unsure. And your dark expressionless eyes listened to my words as you sipped a sweet, round South African wine. And in those many minutes of saying what I wanted to say to you, I heard nothing. You were probably tired from getting stopped by the customs officials (how insulting!), and then again waking up at 4 a.m. would tire anyone out. Or maybe, sad, expecting more–expecting to see me with innocent smiles and unhurried words.

It's just the candlelight flickering here on my balcony, lighting my pen's way in the dark shadows of the late night. My impatiens–the ones you laughed out aloud at as was your custom because they seemed so small and withered, have now blossomed beautifully, with bright blood-red, white and pink flowers exploding, even green vines growing uncontrollably from my pots. I remember how you told me about your prized garden in Monterrey, and how you spent each Sunday there tending to it, as your neighbours would come to look and talk, thinking that their dogs and cats had gone astray near your home. "No, señora..." you'd tell them, and out of kindness you'd chat. Or you reminding me, laughingly: "You go pee like my grandmother!"

And that first night we arrived in Montreal, we made love, half-soaked and steamed from the shower we had together. So much energy had been expended by both of us in just getting there, in getting ourselves ready to see what would happen between us on this trip, that we were deeply quiet after as we held onto each other. And I still remember my words to you as I could not contain the flow of tears, my voice trembling, "I don't want you to lose your mother or your culture," I whispered to you, "as I have lost mine, here..." And your eyes remained silent, so silent that words weren't needed between us. I soon wiped away my tears, tears that held the story of my life. There were many things I did not reveal to you, mi amor. I rather just asked questions of you, and I wanted to learn about your family, the customs of your people and the painful history and joyful music of your country. Even your place in it. And I can recall each rhyming sentence and word, because it was nearly as if in the painful end, I knew I might lose you (as I did). It was as if I had to choose between love and art, laughter and anguish. I wanted to remember every-thing–your smiling mournful eyes, the hand that held your cigarette to your lips a certain way, your slender body and the way it danced, moved–sí, corazón.

It is cold tonight, so cold that I have worn a light sweater and socks. I think I am catching a sniffle, too. The still night is before me, with the city lights echoing in the distance. You must just be finishing at your shop, sweeping the last bit of dark hair from the floor. Or maybe you are taking a break, lighting a cigarette with the lighter I bought for you at the airport, pockets empty. Remember–the one with the red Canadian flag pasted on it? And what about the miniature stuffed grey dolphin to add to your collection, and the book of poetry by Lorca I presented and signed for you? "I will sing these canciones to you," I wrote. Or our memories of us on the busy streets in the village, or during the Festival International de Jazz de Montreal.

It had been so long since I "lived" with someone save for my self. And then you came into my life so beautifully, so suddenly. You reminded me of my first boyfriend, who travelled with me to Cancun twelve years ago. I still remember meeting you at that sunset bar, and the time you invited me to your padre's house, the one he built for your family in Vallarta. You posing, sporting your physique in front of that young banana tree, no taller than you, its large leaves draping over and above, giving you shade. And then that night as we slept together kissing, you jumped up quickly. "I have to remove this!" you said to me. And off you went with a heavy lidded bowl. "I cannot bring dishonour to him!" you blurted out as if talking to yourself, returning to me. It was your father's ashes! I chuckled out loud, thinking you were serious, even humorous. And in Old Montreal when we visited Basilique Notre-Dame with its ancient domed ceilings, a replica of the Basilica in Paris, I made a bit of a joke with you. It was something like, "Let's find a place for us to smooch in here," and you looked very upset with me. Instead, you lit a candle and knelt down, eyes closed to say a quiet prayer to St. Anne–the patron saint of miracles. What miracle were you praying for? Maybe a special ofrenda for your father, who had just passed away? I guess I didn't realize that you still were very Catholic, even though you hated what it said about men like us. Maybe I didn't fully understand your culture, mi amor.

Twenty minutes from Vallarta by motor-boat, I cannot forget our beautiful moment as we watched the sunset in our room at Hotel Lagunita de Yelapa, the breathless bay before us as we noticed the mist quickly descend down from the steep mountains where homes were powered only by fire. All this from our small palapa cabaña and mosquito net draping over the bed and our thatched shutters held open as the palm-leaf roof kept us cool. Or the early night there when we made love in that stone cold shower, as we only felt the water become warm later when the coconuts and gas were put in our heater, just outside our room on that steep slope where we watched the old man put a match to it. We were as happy as two young newlyweds. And you didn't wake me up during the middle of the night when you were ill, when you couldn't breathe after eating that fish dinner. I was frightened for you when I saw you in the morning as we waited for our boat back to Vallarta. I couldn't hold onto you–there were sleepy schoolchildren with us, and the jagged waves kicked on us as the boat bounced up and down as we passed Los Arcos, the sun blinding our tired, hungry faces. The wind tore through us like we were little sticks.

I am now back at my day job, and you are back in Mexico at your hair salon. Can our lives change, mi amor? That is what you wanted, isn't it? That is what I want. When we found each other it was as if that was the moment we wanted. Nearly as if we knew each other before meeting. So briefly it seemed that I was Xochiquetzal to you, the bearer of flowery words. I am the same person, the same writer you met in Vallarta. My love for you and your country and people–those who have struggled against injustice and poverty–have not changed. Maybe I see a similarity between Mexico and South Africa, like those who are dispossessed as the Cape coloureds–my people. You mentioned your Indian blood briefly and I tasted the fullness of your round lips, the way you moved rhythmically to music especially at that dark, smoky nightclub on Rue St. Catherines where we listened and swayed to a Cuban band or two.

Those days with you for two weeks, and the time I met you in Mexico will always remain with me. It was as if you hadn't left. I felt I couldn't just stop calling you after we had that talk on the phone. "Sí, remember I love you," I said to you, my last words. And then you hung up, a señora probably waiting for you to finish with her new hairstyle, you worked so hard to sculpt, to *change* her. But your sudden silence was too harsh for me to bear, too.

We are of the same kind. You and I. The same kind of hombre. Both fatherless, and in a sense, somewhat motherless. Hardworking but also wanting more out of life–and love. You cannot tell you mother about what you do with men, and I was unable to live my life with the woman who gave me life, who would have given my life true meaning. I speak to her at night, ask her questions. But when you were here my conversations with her stopped. Do I have to find love to stop talking to my mother, to stop longing, to stop the pain of mourning–to *live*?

I told you that I saw you in my dreams and wrote of you even before we met. And the sea came to us as our lips touched. I still mourn your absence, mi amor. It's the kind of feeling you get when your mother dies–as if you should cut off all of your hair. You want to crumble, weep as the tides rise. The pain remains, and certain things–rhythmic and desperately sad music–the kind that Mercedes Sosa is known for–her lamenting songs of her nation and people, and the laughter, the music and you trying to teach me Spanish we shared, or even the sound of someone just speaking your language on the busy streets or on the subway somewhere, brings back much emotion. The few bottles of beer you liked to drink cold still remain unopened in my fridge. Everywhere I see a young woman or man with electric blue or wild purple hair–I will see your eyes looking at them. That searching Frida Kaylo stare. Reminding me of my mother's lovely painful hazel eyes, mi amor. And now the future is ahead of us both. Let us take your father's young boat–just us two–in the turquoise ocean teeming with fish, and revel in seeing the first ray of sun off the Isla Mujeres on the eve of the new century.

San Francisco, 1997

The adventurous Leo and Water Tiger in me told me to take my bathing suit off. I felt shy doing so and sat on my towel before I was fully exposed to the sun, the wind, the sand and sea. Yet I didn't mind men looking at me. Most of them were my age: in their thirties. It was the younger ones who kept their long walking shorts on, although they walked shirtless. A cute white buffed man whom I asked to take my photo stopped by.

I asked him to snap me as I sat down exposed on the beach where many men from San Francisco came. The area was directly below the brown Golden Gate Bridge.

"How do you want this shot?" he asked standing shamelessly naked in front of me, and looking directly at my tanned body in more than one way.

"Oh just a regular shot," I said quickly.

He asked if he should take another shot.

"Sure," I answered back.

The man stood back and took one more, handing me my disposable camera. I smiled and said thanks. Then walking away towards the rough grey rocks, he looked around slowly, walked back to the other side of the beach again, following a number of others, behind their tracks. Endless tracks. Nice chest and legs, I thought. A lone figure, he slowly disappeared past other rock forms on the beach into nothingness.

It was already 4 p.m., and I thought that there might easily be another good few hours still. The sun was extremely feverish and water droplets began to run from my neck down to my lower back, caught by the white cotton towel underneath. I laid down and went from my journal to one of the two books I had picked up in the Castro–*Man of My Dreams*, and a special edition of *The Cancer Journals* by Audre Lorde and published by aunt lute books. I read her introduction to *The Cancer Journals*, then came across a brief journal entry that described her early fight with cancer:

> *I want to write rage but all that comes is sadness. We have been*
> *sad long enough to make this earth either weep or grow fertile.*
> *There must be some way to integrate death into living, neither*
> *ignoring it nor giving in to it.*

Lorde took an African name–Gambda Adira–just prior to her death. It means Warrior: She who Makes her Meaning Known. She had finally said that "battling racism, battling heterosexism, and battling apartheid share the same urgency as battling cancer." When Mummy died, in my anger and mourning, I wanted to change my last name to her maiden name, but didn't in the end. An African naming ceremony, like the poet's, would be important, much later. I had felt like I had battled most of my life, too. There was Mummy's final death in November, and my anxious trip to Johannesburg to bury her there. And how hard it had been to get me to San Francisco. The ups and downs of editing *Liberating Minds* over three years. Finding a publisher and sending in the final manuscript. Lorde had felt that it was the love of women who kept her going in finishing her novel during the late 1970s. What would Daddy had thought of my book if he were still here? I reflected back on Isaac who had called me and left a message on my phone: "Thanks for our time at the Riverdale Pool. I'm really trying as hard as I can. And, I hope you know that. Especially if we look back at the past couple of years–because I *do* love you very much. I thought we could explore other ways of seeing our relationship." My bitterness about my relationships with men had subsided over the past few years. I was more at peace with my self, my surroundings. Felt relatively alone despite some men straggling past me. I wasn't there to cruise, just to relax, read and write. Take solace.

I looked into the distant expanse of the ocean. It stood still, like a giant, shiny, smooth mirror. My life had been a whirlwind of activity. One never sat still being a lover of men, even life. I thought back now, to what I had told my first boyfriend over ten years ago: "After we see each other, you'll go back to women, and so will I. In fact, we won't even remember this happened." I was a bit naïve, and wrongheaded. My sexuality, and indeed my race, has been so central to who I was, became. And yes, I had to come to terms with my blackness. As I approach middle-age–whatever that means in gay terms, I want peace, serenity and spiritual fulfilment. I met another coloured gay man at the gym, and think about learning more of him and his family who have even lived on the same street we did back home. It says a lot about me understanding my self, my own culture, now thirteen years after seeing my reflection in the mirror and whom I might still become. But at the same time, I feel that I cannot define my self solely as one who loves my own sex. I am looking for greater wholeness of spirit, mind and body.

As I closed my eyes, the sun glowing all around me, I heard the sound of waves crashing against the shore. *Swoosh. Swoosh.* I wondered if Mummy had heard this soothing sound as she died. Was she in any pain? In her final moment of truth, did her spirit rise from her earthly body, did she feel a magnificent bright light–perhaps her guardian angel–who had been watching over her for these many years, offering her soothing words of consolation, as it glowed radiantly, so that her journey to the other side could begin? In Igbo culture, novelist Onuora Nzekwu has said that "every individual has a chi–a spiritual double and guardian angel, on whom his success or failure in life depended." Like the beloved Lazarus, maybe Mummy was convinced that she would be taken into the presence of God, encircling and radiating upon her, or that the winged Isis, the Egyptian goddess of death-rebirth, was looking over her shoulder.

I had been living with anger for most of my life, the anger of not having a nurturing father. The anger of losing my mother and culture so early in my life, unnaturally. Both are now gone. The wounds inflicted by my parents, I feel, shook me terribly, even threatening my very survival and jeopardizing my trust and sense of self-worth. I was but seven when Mummy "died." And my sisters a few years older. My father seemed to show no pity on the poor woman or her children who mourned for her–always. I couldn't remember him teaching me much but how to work hard, struggle long. He was such an influential role model who seemed to have little to offer me. I have been cracking apart and am tired of blaming my self or them. I have shunned all love, replacing it instead with going to the clubs and baths. I now understand that it is time to begin to forgive them for what happened in the past, to forgive my *self* and tell my parents this somehow.

To forgive is divine, and two metaphors speak of this: God's treading iniquities under foot and God's casting sins into the depths of the sea. In Jeremiah 33:8 God said that "I will purify them of all of their iniquities...and I will forgive all their sins." The parable of the prodigal son also talks about forgiveness: those whom Jesus received, whether they be crushed by illness or guilt or social ostracism, those otherwise shamed, could find freedom in God's forgiving hands. Embracing his son warmly, the forgiving and patient father would celebrate the beginning of a new and closer relationship with the irresponsible son. As a little boy, I had always prayed in Sunday school, "forgive us our debts, as we also have forgiven our debtors." Shutting my eyes, I began to chant these solemn words out repeatedly:

Father, forgive him for he did not know what he was doing.

Forgive me for looking down on my father. Forgive me for not caring more for my mother.

If I forgave, might I find, accept forgiveness?

Father, mother, forgive me.

Maybe it was this unconditional love that I finally needed, desired, and that of a divine force. My presence here was no mere coincidence. The sun beat all around me, the sea and the air cooled my thoughts, and now I felt a glow, a feeling of ecstasy, suddenly overcome me. Something in me had been released, even healed. A silent pause and silence soon came as I took in the pulse of the ocean's tides and the sun's rays on my uncovered and body, free of any material possessions. Eyes closed, I took it and breathed it all in again.

After more time had elapsed, the calm waters pulled me to its shore, and I came across a plastic Coke bottle with a screw-on lid. Maybe I should send what I had written out to sea, I thought. The sun was setting fast on the distant horizon as another outstretched barge streamed up ahead the coast, probably to Asia.

I tore that seven-page letter out of my writing journal, a letter written to myself, and rolled it up into a scroll so that it would fit comfortably in the bottle. The letter–a rejoiceful poem of love and death–fit easily through the bottle's opening. I screwed on its lid. With it now in hand, I walked over to the shore–still naked and feeling nothing but that cool breeze and hot sun on me. A radiating warmth. I held my hand back, took my aim out to sea, and vigorously tossed it and its spiritual contents out into the cold waters of the turquoise blue expanse beyond. And with it I also threw away all of my pills, the ones I had been taking for years. But when I saw the Coke bottle hit the choppy waters my heart fluttered when my right hand came over my forehead to block out the sun so that I could see my throw-away. I imagined that my message of love would drift out to sea, not to be pulled up by someone–if anyone–again for months or even years. Maybe what I had written was indecipherable to anyone save my self. In a sense, I felt as though I had thrown my troubles away, cleansing and purifying my soul. The final act of a rocky and arduous journey on earth.

Perhaps an act of forgiveness to my self, this act would try to unravel the insanity of my life. It would have said that life was too short. I had lost that deep spiritual connection in my self by searching for sex, *not* love. But many men did not know how to love. I had been lost for too long. And now I truly wanted something more in life. To recreate my self spritually: maybe find someone significant. After all, we black gay and bisexual men and lesbians had re-recreated ourselves many times over, *with* or *without* our families, and succeeded at it. We were always searching, wandering flames, walking on the earth's fragile surface. Fear from continuing rejection, abandonment, ridicule, isolation and loneliness–even eternal damnation–threatened us more than anything else. If only we could overcome this.

I wanted that message to reach my parents. To tell them that I was still alive, that my life was worth living, that I had forgiven not only my self, but them too. My body remembered my mother's pain. Her death was my resurrection. Life became a blessing, not a curse. Now I wanted to wash the anguish in my life away. Replenish it with fresh cool rain water. I had gotten to know them better since they had died, and even though my mother had been gone just a few months, I had been living with her death and life's memory–mourning and rejoicing her life through my own, and my sisters. Isaac was still in Toronto. We talked from time to time. I still looked after the first, second and third sisters too, just as my dad had in his own difficult way. Carrying on the family's name. But the flame was anew; it took on a brighter, divine glow.

I packed my things away into my small bright red knapsack and got dressed. It was 5:20 but the sun's rays were still intense. As I walked back up the beach, trying to find the place where the path would lead me back to the cliff top and eventually to the bus stop, I came across an old Spanish fisherman perched between two fishing rods stuck high into the sand with their lines cast out to sea. Fully clothed, wearing high fisherman's boots, he showed me his catch of the day. "It's still my life here, me and the fish," he said to me, half jokingly. He must have realized that there were men here walking around without clothes on. But that didn't bother him. He just kept right on fishing. I waved good-bye, treasuring the little slice of life he had expressed to me in my few seconds of knowing him. Then I walked up to the bottom of the face of the cliff and finally found my path. Looking back at the man and the beauty of the sea, I turned around and let out a sigh as I peered up the steep face of the cliff. *Would I be able to make it up, again?* Life was like a path. Going up and down, leading somewhere. Eventually we found ourselves, crossing many rivers, some roaring and others shallow.

I found surer footing on one of the sharp rocks that rose from the path a few steps up, and pressed on. Mother Africa reached out and smiled warmly upon her native son.

The Family: An Excerpt

*Winter. The Family Café. A greasy spoon dive on Queen Street opposite a psychi-
atric institution for long-term patients. The food here is cheap and tasteless. Its
smoky environment makes the main character, a young man, uneasy. Poverty
abounds. The café's decor is not bright, but dark and uninviting with cheap wall
murals and plastic plants. The young man is here to visit one of his sisters with the
eldest sister. He reminisces about their lives, past and present.*

YOUNG MAN

Ja, Grace. You left out the part that Daddy was *just* a garbageman. That he drank
himself to sleep every night... That the condo was rented, and that he kicked you out
most of the time, clothes and all. I still remember him on that smoke-filled couch,
with a body mark from him sitting, watching television and reading the newspaper all
of the time. The same couch he slept on after drinking, getting up sober as a tiger to
start work again each morning. It destroyed him, and it destroyed me watching him
each time. But he didn't allow us to talk openly about Mummy's absence in the
house, her illness or ours, and he would always say to the neighbours that she had
died. I mean, that is such a monstrous and insensitive thing to say in front of a child.
About Mummy. I hated him from that moment on, and just the way he would treat
me knowing I was different and all. I thought if he died I wouldn't shed a tear. No, I
wouldn't. But when I was called by the nurse from the hospital at 5 a.m. to hear the
news of his death, I told her not to remove his body from his bed. I had felt so
awfully guilty because the night before when I was to visit him I was with a friend–a
woman, and later, we had sex. No, I had deflowered her. Felt even more guilty about
this, that I should have been by his side, saying good-bye, looking into his eyes. I
took a cab there within minutes of hearing of his passing away, even driving by the
first building where we lived next to the highway. Remember that old run-down
place where we stayed with other coloured families? I thought about Mummy, her
not coming with us. That was our whole life here in this blaady cold place.
Mummy–not coming with us. I was the first to arrive at the hospital. And when I
looked at him in his bed, I removed the sheet and saw him there lying naked in front
of me. The first time that I could remember seeing him like this, with nothing in
between us. He had aged but was relaxed, content. No longer with us. He was no
longer *with* us. I felt it was useless to be angry with him and that it might take me
much more time to forgive, too, to get over our vicious arguments and deathly
silence. But then I went to him, held him tightly, as if he were my only brother,
caressing him gently in his passing. Looked at him one final time, and let him down
gently, my shaking fingers brushing his closed eyes and the gentle slope of his mouth.
Then you people came. Brenda was too afraid to even touch him; she left the room.
I cried for him, as if all my anger had turned to a sea of love. I cried for my life. For
Mummy and for all of us, Kathy. But it always comes back to you, Gracie–meisie.
That's what Daddy used to call you, isn't it? "Meisie, make Daddy some tea," and
you'd run to do it, to give it to him in the living room. Then you'd quickly leave his
presence, careful not to bump into anything or break it. The house was silent from
the moment he walked in the door from work. A kind of deathly silence that never
leaves or escapes you. Do you remember that?

104

To Whom It May Concern

21st April, 1967

I have known and worked with Him for the past twenty-seven years, and have been
Secretary to him in our foremost South African Coloured Cricket Association, and
also in the Diamond Fields Cricket Union, both of which he has been President of for
many years now. He is a highly respected Commissioner of Oaths.

and he remembered this, displaying that wooden plaque proudly on his bedroom wall
in the country in which he hoped to win both he and his children their freedom and a
new life

This man has impressed me with his initiative, diligence, perseverance and integrity
in everything he undertakes, and these qualities have always brought his success.

and he remembered this, always putting a roof over their heads with food, clothing

This man has been a loyal, competent and efficient employee of the De Beers
Consolidated Mines Ltd., where he is still employed, and where his services are
greatly valued. Seeking to create a better world, he is the organizer of all social functions, and our community holds him in very high esteem, because he is the leading
official of over fourteen welfare organizations, as well as being the Chairman of the
Transvaal Road Primary School, Chairman of the Thistles Rugby Club, Chairman of
the Beaconsfield Wanderers Cricket Club and auditer of the South African Rugby
Union.

and he remembered this, talking each friday night over drinks with his older brother
of the old country and the family and friends who were still there, living the crisis

His untiring efforts in the administration and organizing of all functions and events
that lead to the educational and cultural uplift of his community have always been
successful, because he is a born organizer and administrator, with a pleasing and
attractive, yet forceful, personality.

and he remembered this, seeing the very same traits in his only son whom he loved so

Coming from a very highly respected family, he is a loyal and devoted member of the
Anglican Church, where his services on various committees of the church are very
much appreciated.

and he remembered this, taking his young children to church each sunday, without her

He will be a grave *loss* to a community that loses him, and a very valuable gain to
one that accepts him. He bears with him my personal best wishes for every success
in the future.

and he lived this, each day.

Self-Portrait of the Artist, 2032

The rains and wind came down furiously for the third straight day. This was my first visit to Serowe–the village of the rainwind–and Bessie Head's home, where I walked through the place where she scribbled down her notes for her novels. The gravesite is close by at Botolaote cemetary, and for the past two days I have visited it and the Khama III Memorial Museum where her papers are housed. There are many water-soaked flowers placed at the grave, from many noteworthy people, admiring friends and other writers. The place overlooks the Serowe plain and it is sandy, stony, with weeds growing here and there. Head had wanted her grave to remain unmarked, and as with the local custom, I have learned it is important to place a red stone from those lying about upon it. Then my fresh-cut flowers. How might her characters have spoken to her? What did this lonely place mean to her while she still struggled with life over and over again with her young son, while the white masters of apartheid furiously ruled next door?

Wintertime in Cape Town. The long stretches of beaches are bare, and no one is dressed in shorts. The sea comes up to tickle my feet a bit, but I soon have to leave the cool waters at the lip of the beachfront. I remember to take more photographs of District Six, and many more coloureds, Africans and tourists are visiting the area than ever before. The houses of the children and their children whose parents and grandparents were removed by force from the bulldozed area now dot the landscape from all around. The coloureds have renewed their future with the building of monuments to their history here. Local cafés on Hanover Street, close to the old Hanover Street of the old days, feature a host of jazz musicians, other artists and poets nearly nightly. I even remember some of my past glories and people asked me to take part, and so I do. How beautiful to listen to their lyrical words–a mix of Afrikaans, English and the many other indigenous languages, and for them to want to hear my own voice. There is plenty of laughter and tears, and my heart and belly are happy for it.

I have for many years come home to visit both Kimberley, where my father's ashes are entombed at his parents' grave, as well as to see Jo'burg. The country is doing well and is more prosperous than ever before. The generation that was born just after democracy has its own children now. And speaking to some of these people, I can see that they will lead the country to its renewed future. At his parents' small grave, I stayed at Daddy's side, tended the flowers and thought about him, even Mummy. Back in Canada, I had gone through some old family photos, and found one of me as a young newborn, smiling, diapered, head propped up as I lay kicking with life on the settee in our house. On the back of the snap of me, Daddy wrote: *To my godfather, with all of my love. "I am three months old today."* Maybe my father knew I was going to see Mummy because the sun suddenly came out so brilliantly over the sad heavy clouds, as if he or some larger-than-life thing, an unreckoned natural force, said I'd be there. As I arrived at the Jo'burg airport, I met John, much older, with two of his grandchildren. I hugged him and them. They were big and smiling as children are, clinging by and hugging his side.

Today was close to my second birthday. We are born every thirty-five years (I have only realized this after reflecting on my parents' lives after their death). I am now the age my father was when he passed away, but my health, at least physically, is on my side. Last month was the sixty-sixth anniversary of the Soweto Riots (Daddy left us, at least physically, on its eighteenth anniversary), and the crowds and those who came to the various functions in Jo'burg and elswhere–the grandchildren of those who were gunned down–still remembered the stories, the tragedy, and now the wonder of life. South Africa was a sight to behold, and I've noticed that the streets are filled with couples mixing from all races. Africa is no longer at war with itself, and poverty and illness is decreasing.

I am more excited by life's offerings, and the visit to Mummy's grave was a moment I always cherished, wanted to photograph, at least mentally. The time I held her casket to place it in the hard earth was still with me as if it were just yesterday.

Somewhere, I have a photo of my mother and her sister at my oupa and ouma's gravesite, here at this place. They are standing grey and stone-faced. The lone trees in the background have now reached into the sky so that the mine dumps in the flat distance do not come to mind. Looking at the tombstone I asked to be raised at Mummy's grave, I still remembered the few but memorable words I wanted inscribed. It was on the blessing of her life, of living, of not forgetting, always remembering: it simply said that she had lived as a much-loved mother, wife, daughter and sister of Africa. My sisters, much older, gave me something to read to her. I was with Mummy for a long, long time. As I poured out some water on her grave because I remembered how she could not swallow anything before her passing, I said: *I am you and him, and I think you wanted me to be strong like the earth for the other three because I am the only remaining man of the family.* My words were a libation of freedom and love. My hand took the red earth and I smelled its rich, red, curried, dry scent, the wind on the veld picking up to lick me. Was it her, speaking back to me gently, knowingly? Does she know that I *am*, that I have always been *with* her? I do not cry for her as often as I did many years ago. But tears still have memory.

In Toronto, his strong African sculptor's hands and young heart waits for me. I have picked up some things for him, special small gifts that only he knows their delicate meaning, scent. Even rooibos tea, and certain spices, the splendid aroma he remembers. She hugged me tightly at the Toronto airport before leaving. We stayed in each other's arms forever; the crowd stood still, watching us. *The drums beat. Everything about her is me; everything about me is her.*

Another of my films is all but complete. There is a bit of my family in it, and my sisters voices are there, too. Mummy lives in the way the sky mixes in with the multicoloured high-veld, in the scent of the flowers now exploding in the Cape, or as the clouds descend over Table Mountain in the early morning hours. So, too, is Daddy–his strong hands, his silent unknownness and the arresting beauty of his halting, firm and intelligent voice. I remember that the man smiled, too. The landscape of my home country is beautifully photographed in it–again. But this time, the plot is less complex, the characters speak poetically about their lives–not of escaping from harrowing worlds, but of simply living, of breathing, seeing, even sensing and wanting love, desiring some kind of beautiful meaning to their lives, to life. Desiring to see the world more just, at peace. Desiring to *live*, be free.

NOTES

xi, The estimated coloured population of South Africa (1998) was 3.7 million (8.8 percent of the total population) of roughly 2.8 million were in the Eastern and Western provinces. Linda Van Buren, "South Africa: Economy," in *Africa South of the Sahara 2000*, 29th edition (London: Europa, 2000), 1014. *The Group Areas Act* of 1950 (amended in 1966) revealed the problematic way in which coloured citizens were legally defined, subordinated and separated socially, politically and ethnically by the white hegemonic state during apartheid. For example, a "coloured group included (i) any person who is not a member of the white group or of the native group; and (ii) any woman, to whichever race, tribe, or class she may belong, between whom a person who is, in terms of subparagraph (i), a member of the coloured group, there exists a marriage, or who cohabitats with such a person; (iii) any white man between whom a woman who in terms of sub-paragraph (i) is a member a member of the coloured group, there exists a marriage, or who cohabitats with such a woman." And Proclamation 123 of 1967 divided coloured people further in the following categories: (1) Cape coloured; (2) Malay; (3) Griqua; (4) Chinese; (5) Indian; (6) "other" Asiatic; (7) "other" coloured. For futher reading on "apartheid," "otheredness," the "post-colonial body" and "post-colonialism" see: Bill Ashcroft et al., eds., *Key Concepts in Post-Colonial Studies* (London: Routledge, 1998), 17-20, 169-173, 183-195.

xii, The *Daily Mail and Guardian* in October of 1999 reported that the ANC government intended to ban "'hurtful words' such as 'kaffir,' 'boer,' 'meid' ('whore' for mixed race women), 'hotnot' (short form for hottentot and made fun of coloureds), 'coon' and 'coolie,' (used to describe Indians) as well as 'bobbejaan' (used in Afrikaans to chastise blacks)." This draconian piece of legislation that was to combat racial discrimination had civil rights and artistic groups in arms because it contravened the present constitution. McGreal, Chris. (1999). ANC to outlaw "hurtful" words. In *Daily Mail & Guardian* [online]. Available: http://www.mg.co.za/mg/news/99oct1/8oct-language.html [1999, October 8].

xii, Moffies, ngochani, moataona, bulldagger, anti-man, batty man, zami–all are names given to, adopted and reclaimed by "queers" in the (South) African and Caribbean diaspora. Also cited on that page: "Africa," by Vivian Derryck and Robert J. Berg, in George T. Kurian and Graham T. T. Molitor, eds., *Encyclopedia of the Future* (London: Simon & Schuster and Prentice Hall International, 1996), Vol. 1, 10.

2-10, *i, blanche*. Blanche's escape through dreams are based on the Khoisan ritual of dance and trance-like states. As well, Stephen Watson's poetry collection, *Return of the Moon* (Cape Town: Carrefour Press, 1991), uniquely attempts to translate the many stories of three /Xam or Khoisan "convicts," who lived with W. H. Bleek, a German linguist, who settled in Cape Town in the 1850s and learned and translated their language he knew would be lost due to the the destruction and killing of the /Xam by white colonialists. Various poems in the collection were examined, which are *solely* Watson's poetic interpretation, to understand the dying culture of the Khoisan population, the coloured people's ancestors. Religious quote, p. 6, excerpted from *My Prayer Book: A Book of Private Devotions. Authorized by the Bishops of the Province of S. Africa for use therein* (London: Longmans, 1952), 84.

15-17, *coloured days, coloured days*. European fascination and historical sexual objectification of the "hottentot's women's bodies," are revealed in: Sander L. Gilman, *Difference and Pathology: Stereotypes of Sexuality, Race and Madness* (Ithaca, New York: Cornell University Press, 1985), 88-89.

19-21, *the place we come from*. Vernon A. February, *Mind Your Colour: The "Coloured"*

108

Stereoptype in South African Literature (London: Kegan Paul International, 1991), 103.

22, *Dearest Mummy*. Godparents were and still are important to coloured family life. They promised to help teach their adopted godchildren the ways of the Christian church over a thirteen-to-fourteen-year time period. See: *My Prayer Book*, 73.

24, *she moved*. "Kaffir-lover" was and is a South African derogatory term, akin to "nigger lover."

29, *narrative of sister januarie, 1826*. The fact that slaves were drunk has been recorded, but what many early European scholars did not conclude was that the burgher-masters would give them drink or dop, perpetuating this and hence stereotyping coloureds as always being drunken. J. S. Marais' *The Cape Coloured People, 1652-1937* (New York: AMS Press, 1978) notes the former (p. 44). He specifically looks at the period before emancipation to investigate where coloureds derived their "present day" culture–that of their slave past. Historically, in the eighteenth century, European men took non-European women as wives without church marriage, yet the burgher father rarely declared his coloured child as legitimate lest he could inherit the father's property. Vrije burghers or free burghers established the first white farms in South Africa and pourboire was the wine money given by the master to his male slaves on Saturdays.

39-43, *from here to district six*. SLEG BLANKES in Afrikaans means "Europeans Only" and these soul-destroying and destructive words were posted on signs everywhere in South Africa during apartheid to restrict non-whites from white areas, including beaches, libraries, swimming pools, parks, public transit, public washrooms and many other places and facilities. It was a constant reminder that one's race defined one's status or lack of status in society. "the food tasting like urine...maim, kill again," refers to the assassination by Demitrio Tsafendas (1918-1999) of Hendrik Verwoerd, State President and architect of apartheid. South Africa's political history changed radically after.

55, *here/now*. "e," is the short form for ecstasy, ethylenedioxmethamphetamine, a "rave drug," that exploded into the gay subculture in the mid to late 1990s. "g," known as GHB, gamma hydroxy butyrate, is a tranquilizer that can be taken in a clear liquid form to induce light drunkenness. Similarly, Special K, or "k," ketamine hydrochloride, was snorted or smoked to enduce a hallucinogenic trance. Men used these at dance clubs, especially circuit parties.

59, *fear the living, not the dead*. Amalia Rodriguez was known for introducing fado music to her native Portugal and the world. These sad, haunting, traditional songs combined Arab, African and Portuguese cultures. Fado means "fate" in Portuguese.

61, *and yet another prescription from my shrink*. Medical information quoted in part I excerpted from: Fred F. Ferri, *Practical Guide to the Care of the Patient* (St. Louis: C. V. Mosby Company, 1987), 495.

62-64, *at 27*. *Maru* was novelist Bessie Head's second great literary accomplishment. Her white mother whom she never knew had been branded insane for associating and sexually mixing with a black stablehand, whom Head never met. She left South Africa on a one-way exit permit with her young son for Botswana in the early 1960s, and refused to see herself as a "political writer." Harold Head, the author's husband, moved to Toronto and soon edited *Bushman's Brew*, published in 1974 under the nom de plume, Morena Kichwa. Even the title lends itself to African ideas and aspirations. Inspiring and ground-breaking, it was one of the first noteworthy black Canadian literary anthologies and would feature the award-winning Trinidadian-Canadian poet, filmmaker and novelist Dionne Brand. Oshun, in the Yoruba-diasporic pantheon, is associated with the sensual love of women loving women.

70-74, *my black "queer" body.* I am looking for greater "unity" and attempting to use the word "queer" here to go beyond the restricted Western notion that arises from claiming a gay, lesbian, bisexual, transvestite or transgendered "identity," "body," and/or body politic. The great difficulty most black and Third World writers and academics have faced in writing and theorizing about their same sex desire is not only of their displacement from their country of origin, but their racial and sexual oppression in many different ways and forms, some too numerous to define on paper. This short piece is only a partial reflection of my same sex desire, and it originated from a larger essay found in my unpublished manuscript, *I, Moffie: A Queer South African Memoir of Longing, Madness, Love and Desire.* AYA is derived from the Ghanian symbol of defiance and resistance, the fern. Translated, the word also means, "I fear none." The following monographs were used elsewhere in the autobiographical essay's arguments: Robert Mapplethorpe, *Mapplethorpe* (New York: Random House,1992), 335; Franz Fanon, *Black Skin, White Masks* (New York: Grove, 1967), 170; Wesley Crichlow, "Migration, Identity and Black Same-Sex Consciousness," in Debbie Douglas, et. al., eds., *MÁ-KA, Diasporic Juks: Contemporary Writing by Queers of African Descent* (Toronto: Sister Vision Press, 1997), 100-113; Mark Gevisser and Edwin Cameron, eds., *Defiant Desire: Gay and Lesbian Lives in South Africa* (New York: Routledge, 1995), xiii; Henry Louis Gates Jr,. *Thirteen Ways of Looking at a Black Man* (New York: Random House, 1997), 62-63.

76, *hear meee brotha.* Jah (Hebrew Yah) is a short form of Jahveh (Jehovah). It is the name of God most commonly used by the Rastafarians of Jamaica, a religious group who spurn Western culture.

81, *What's Wrong with Jack Lewis's Film "Dragging at the Roots"*? This letter was sent to the Arts Editor of *Xtra*! but remained unpublished. Dr. Rozena Maart who also attended the screening of the film was outspoken in her furor with Lewis because he didn't seem to know certain historical truths about the demise of District Six or when the last families were forcibly removed even though he had produced the film. At the same time, the filmmaker was completely caught off-guard by the amount of criticism coming from the audience after the screening.

85, *petals weep but the rose lives eternally.* From 1990 to 1997 it was estimated that Canada sold $3, 107, 345 worth of military equipment to the Indonesian military, which terrorized and killed the East Timorese until the arrival of UN peacekeepers in late September of 1999. *Now Magazine*, September 16-22, 1999, letter to the editor, 14.

91, *Pensée.* The *War Measures Act* was invoked by Canadian Prime Minister Pierre Elliott Trudeau in the October 1970 crisis after the kidnapping of British trade commissioner James Cross and Quebec cabinet minister Pierre Laporte (who was later killed) by the separatist group Front de Liberation du Quebec.

92, *untitled: 7.6.99.* Xochipilli is the Aztec god of flowers and sensual pleasures.

95, *of human truth and injustice.* I created this piece by looking at the various demands for basic human rights of the indigenous peoples by the Zapatista Army during the Chiapas uprising in 1994 against the Mexican government for greater socio-economic and political independence due to their oppression and impoverishment that came about especially as a result of the signing of the Canada-U.S. Free Trade Agreement. This poem is a "found poem," one in which the poet "finds" a truthful and related meaning of his text to another text.

96-98, *attends-moi.* Xochiquetzal is the Aztec goddess and patron of poets. Frida Kahlo (1907-

1954) was one of Mexico's most important and vital painters of the twentieth century. Kahlo's surrealist self-portraits in which she wore the traditional costume of the Tuhuana women revealed the deep physical and spiritual pain of her life and deal with the complex themes emerging from Mexico's colonized and native past as well as its rise to modern industrialism after its post-revolutionary period. Mexicans revere her as a true nationalist.

99-102, *San Francisco, 1997.* Audre Lorde, *The Cancer Journals* (San Francisco, California: aunt lute books, 1997), 11.

GLOSSARY

A Note: The foreign-language terms used in this glossary may have other related and inter-related meanings. I have attempted to use these terms in the manner in which they are defined here. Foreign language terms were not italicized in the text because I believe that they are of equal value to–*not* lesser value–than English. Each post-colonial writer is limited also by the way he or she remembers their use in his or her particular culture, or by the way other rich cultures may speak or give meaning to their intricate languages.

Africville	impoverished and demolished black community in Nova Scotia that was moved by the white municipal government to large-scale public housing in the 1960s; still viewed as an outrageous act of racism by black Nova Scotians and African Canadians
Afrikaans	derivative of Dutch language spoken mostly by Afrikaners and coloureds; one of the main eleven national languages in South Africa along with English and other indigenous languages
Afrikaners	descendants of Dutch, German and French settlers in South Africa
abuela	grandmother (Spanish)
ag	oh; exclamatory (Afrikaans)
amigo	friend (Spanish)
ANC	African National Congress
apartheid	adopted by the National Party and legally enshrined in 1948, separating people in South Africa by race; nationally and internationally condemned and officially ending with the release of Nelson Mandela from prison in 1990
APO	African Political (later Peoples') Organization; Dr. Abdullah Abdurahman, a Cape Muslim and influential figure in coloured politics, was its founder
assegai	short stabbing spear, introduced by Shaka for the Zulu armies (Afrikaans)
attends-moi	wait for me (French)
AYA	a political and social organization of black gay and bisexual men in Toronto, founded in 1990 and preceded by another group called Zami
Azania	a name first used by the Pan Africanist Congress to refer to South Africa, becoming a Black Consciousness protest name for South Africa
baas	master or boss (Afrikaans)
ban	publications, people and movements could be banned or outlawed under apartheid
banjee boy	homeboy or working class black gay man (African American slang)
batty man	offensive Caribbean term for gay men; reclaimed depending upon whom is using it
besos	kisses (Spanish)
biltong	meat cured by the sun and eaten as a snack by many South Africans (Afrikaans)
Boere	Afrikaners but commonly used as slang for right-wingers or policemen (Afrikaans)
boetie	an affectionate term for a boy child (Afrikaans)
Black Consciousness Movement	led by Steve Biko; banned in 1977, it argued that blacks (including coloureds and Asians) had to liberate themselves and could not rely on whites
braai	barbecue; grilled meat (Afrikaans)
canciones	songs (Spanish)
C.O.	Commissioner of Oaths, nearly akin to Justice of the Peace
coloureds	a mixed group of Malay, African, Khoisan, and European people in South Africa
corazón	heart; darling (Spanish)
dagga	marijuana
District Six	the sixth district in the municipality of Cape Town, overlooking Table Bay; it was the most multiracial residential area in South Africa until it was demolished and declared a "white area" under the Group Areas Act (1950); great bitterness had been caused by the mass removal of mostly coloureds from the area
Gauteng	used by the Basotho to denote Johannesburg, the Witerwatersrand or even South Africa; Sesotho name meaning "Place of Gold," which became the official name of the province that includes Johannesburg and the Witwatersrand that was once the Transvaal

GLOW	Gay and Lesbian Organization of the Witwatersrand; founded by Tseko Simon Nkoli when Nelson Mandela was still in prison, it was the first non-racial gay and lesbian organization in the Witwatersrand; part of the mass democratic movement against apartheid
gringo	foreigner, but especially applies to Americans scornfully (Latin American Spanish)
hijras	eunuchs or castrated men in India; also known to be transvestic and transsexual prostitutes
hlobonga	external intercourse using the inner thighs (Zulu)
hoer	prostitute; whore (Afrikaans)
hombre	man (Spanish)
Hotnots	"Hottentots"; an offensive term for coloureds
Inkatha	mainly Zulu political party and organization
isangoma	diviner; spiritual healer (Zulu)
isibongo	praise song or poetry chanted in honour of a chief or king (Zulu)
Isla Mujeres	Island of the Women, situated off the coast of Cancun, Mexico (Spanish)
ja	yes (Afrikaans)
Jo'burg	Johannesburg
juegos infantiles	child's play (Spanish)
kaffir	nigger; an offensive term for blacks (Afrikaans)
Khoisan	invented general name for both Khoi and San groups of southern Africa; predated arrival of whites and black Africans; reside in Namibia and southwestern Cape area
Kimberley	a city in South Africa, in the province of Northern Cape; it has been a diamond-mining centre since the early 1870s, with the mining of the Big Hole, now a tourist attraction
kinders	children (Afrikaans)
koeksister	a traditional Cape delicacy of Malay origin: a deep-fried twisted doughnut dipped in syrup
kraal	enclosure for farm animals (Afrikaans)
lekker	sweet, delicious or enjoyable (Afrikaans)
letsoku	a mixture of red clay and animal fat circumcised boys of the Pedi prepare for the final stage of male initiation
lettie	lesbian
limosneros	beggars (Latin American Spanish)
madiba	leader; father of the nation (Xhosa); South Africans fondly referred to Nelson Mandela as "madiba" when he was State President
malunde	homeless street children
maricón	queer (Latin American Spanish, offensive, slang)
mealie meal	ground maize; porridge and a staple of food for many South Africans
meisie	an affectionate term for a girl child (Afrikaans)
mi amor	my love (Spanish)
mine dump	a large hill of solidified crushed quartz from which gold has been extracted; a dominate feature in and around Johannesburg where gold mining has taken place
mlandwana	illegitimate child (Zulu)
moeder	mother (Afrikaans)
moffie	"queer" (slang); sometimes a male transvestite; coined by the Cape coloureds
mon amour	my love (French)
mooi	pretty (Afrikaans)
mosadi	woman; a female attaining the status of being a woman once married and having born a child (Pedi)
mucho	very (Spanish)
naai	screw; screwing (Afrikaans)
naar	sick (Afrikaans)
naartjie	tangerine or mandarine orange (Afrikaans)
Nat	member of the National Party
né	"Isn't that so?" (Afrikaans)
niños	children; boys (Spanish)
no gracias	no thank you (Spanish)
non	no (French)
Nongqause	in the 1850s a young Xhosa woman phrophecized that the Xhosa people should purify themselves by killing all cattle, destroying all grain and planting no crops; ancestors would then rise up from the dead and a great wind would sweep all whites and unbelieving blacks into the sea

ofrenda	offering (Spanish)
Oka	place in which First Nations People rebelled in Quebec to secure their land rights; seen as an act of nationalism but put down by the Canadian government through its armed forces
ou	bloke (Afrikaans)
oui	yes (French)
ouma	grandmother (Afrikaans)
oupa	grandfather (Afrikaans)
ousie	respectful term for African woman (Afrikaans)
padre	father (Spanish)
Parti Québécois	Quebec's political party, founded in 1968 and dedicated to achieving Quebec sovereignty
pensée	thinking (French)
rand	currency used in South Africa
Riel, Louis	leader who headed the rebellion of the Métis at Red River Settlement (now Manitoba) in 1869; later wrongly executed by the Canadian state after leading the Northwest Rebellion
rue	street (French)
SABC	South African Broadcasting Corporation; state-owned television and radio services
settee	sofa
señor	mister (Spanish)
señora	Mrs. (Spanish)
señorita	miss (Spanish)
shebeen	establishment selling liquor illegally (township slang)
shrink	psychiatrist (English, slang)
sí	yes (Spanish)
sister	graduate nurse, usually the senior member of a nursing team (South African English)
sjambok	hard leather whip (Afrikaans)
skaam	embarrassed, shy (Afrikaans)
Soweto	the acronym for South West Townships; with a population of 3 million, this giant township is located southwest of Johannesburg
squeegees	the many young homeless youth who work and struggle to make a wage by washing car windows on the streets of Toronto, Montreal and New York
stabane	"queer" (township slang) but also understood to mean "hermaphrodite"
taal	language (Afrikaans)
ubuntu	human-heartedness; the way to relate to people is all important (Zulu)
vader	father (Afrikaans)
Vallarta	Puerto Vallarta, Mexico
veld	field; grasslands on a plateau in South Africa (Afrikaans)
verkragting	rape (Afrikaans)
Xhosa	second largest indigenous group in South Africa; also its language
yoni	the Hindu figure or representation of the female genitals as a sacred spiritual symbol
zami	offensive Caribbean term for lesbian; reclaimed by such luminaries as poet Audre Lorde
Zulu	largest indigenous group in South Africa; also its language